Arduino Robotic Projects

Build awesome and complex robots with the
power of Arduino

Richard Grimmett

[PACKT] open source *
PUBLISHING   community experience distilled

BIRMINGHAM - MUMBAI

Arduino Robotic Projects

First published: August 2014

Production reference: 1070814

Published by Packt Publishing Ltd.
Livery Place
35 Livery Street
Birmingham B3 2PB, UK.

ISBN 978-1-78398-982-9

www.packtpub.com

Cover image by Maria Cristina Caggiani (mariacristinacaggiani@virgilio.it)

Credits

Author
Richard Grimmett

Reviewers
Jimmy Hedman
Pradumn Joshi
Sudar Muthu
Karan Thakkar

Commissioning Editor
Julian Ursell

Acquisition Editor
Sam Wood

Content Development Editor
Akshay Nair

Technical Editors
Manal Pednekar
Ankita Thakur

Copy Editors
Alisha Aranha
Roshni Banerjee
Gladson Monteiro
Karuna Narayanan
Adithi Shetty

Project Coordinators
Mary Alex
Akash Poojary

Proofreaders
Maria Gould
Paul Hindle

Indexers
Hemangini Bari
Mehreen Deshmukh
Rekha Nair
Tejal Soni

Graphics
Sheetal Aute
Ronak Dhruv
Disha Haria
Abhinash Sahu

Production Coordinator
Alwin Roy

Cover Work
Alwin Roy

About the Author

Richard Grimmett has always been fascinated by computers and electronics from his very first programming project that used FORTRAN on punch cards. He has a Bachelor's and Master's degree in Electrical Engineering and a PhD in Leadership Studies. He also has 26 years of experience in the Radar and Telecommunications industries and even has one of the original brick phones. He now teaches Computer Science and Electrical Engineering at Brigham Young University-Idaho, where his office is filled with his many robotic projects. He has authored two books, *BeagleBone Robotic Projects* and *Raspberry Pi Robotic Projects*, for Packt Publishing.

I would certainly like to thank my wife, Jeanne, and my family for providing me with a wonderful, supportive environment that encourages me to take on projects like this one. I would also like to thank my students; they show me that amazing things can be accomplished by those who are unaware of all the barriers.

About the Reviewers

Jimmy Hedman is a professional high performance computing (HPC) geek who works with large systems where size is measured in number of racks and cores. In his spare time, he goes in the opposite direction and focuses on smaller things, such as BeagleBone Blacks and Arduinos. He is currently employed by South Pole AB, the biggest computer server manufacturer in Sweden, where he is a Linux consultant with HPC as his main focus. This is the first book Jimmy has worked on, but hopefully not the last.

I would like to thank my understanding wife who lets me go on with my hobbies like I do. I would also like to thank Packt Publishing for letting me have this much fun with interesting stuff to read and review, and not to forget, Stockholm Robotförening (Stockholm Robot Club), which opened my eyes to how easy it is to actually build a robot.

Pradumn Joshi is currently pursuing his Bachelor's degree in Electrical Engineering from NIT, Surat. He is an avid elocutionist, tinkerer, and debate enthusiast. He is also interested in economics, freelance writing, and western music. His area of technical interest lies in open source hardware development and embedded systems.

I would like to thank my best friends and brothers, Rahul and Parikshit.

Sudar Muthu builds robots as a hobby, and Arduino is his playground. He discovered the joy of hardware programming through Arduino around 4 years back, and since then, he has been using it for his various pet projects. He has created a lot of libraries for Arduino and also currently maintains a Makefile for Arduino that helps you do professional Arduino development.

He conducts workshops about Arduino and robotics and has given talks at various conferences about hardware programming. He blogs about his experience in hardware programming and also about his various projects at `http://hardwarefun.com`.

> I would like to dedicate this book to my parents, who gave me life, to my wife, who made it happier, and to my son, Arul, who made it worth living.

Karan Thakkar is a hybrid mobile developer at Tata Consultancy Services Ltd., with experience in a variety of enterprise projects based on cross-platform frameworks/libraries such as EnyoJS, Sencha Touch, Backbone.js, and PhoneGap. He graduated from Shivaji University with a degree in Electronics and Telecommunication. His blog can be found at `http://karanjthakkar.wordpress.com/blog/`. He has written a couple of interesting and highly viewed articles on OpenCV and Arduino. Being a robotics enthusiast, he rarely stops boasting about how he had the chance to tinker with the humanoid robot, Aldebaran Nao, during an internship.

www.PacktPub.com

Support files, eBooks, discount offers, and more

You might want to visit www.PacktPub.com for support files and downloads related to your book.

Did you know that Packt offers eBook versions of every book published, with PDF and ePub files available? You can upgrade to the eBook version at www.PacktPub.com and as a print book customer, you are entitled to a discount on the eBook copy. Get in touch with us at service@packtpub.com for more details.

At www.PacktPub.com, you can also read a collection of free technical articles, sign up for a range of free newsletters and receive exclusive discounts and offers on Packt books and eBooks.

http://PacktLib.PacktPub.com

Do you need instant solutions to your IT questions? PacktLib is Packt's online digital book library. Here, you can access, read and search across Packt's entire library of books.

Why subscribe?

- Fully searchable across every book published by Packt
- Copy and paste, print and bookmark content
- On demand and accessible via web browser

Free access for Packt account holders

If you have an account with Packt at www.PacktPub.com, you can use this to access PacktLib today and view nine entirely free books. Simply use your login credentials for immediate access.

Table of Contents

Preface

We live in a wonderful time where we have access to marvelous chunks of technology that inspire our creativity. The personal computer, smart phone, web cam – all of these make our lives easier, but more importantly, more creative. These new inventions invite us to not only become users, but also developers and creators, adding our own adaptions to the wide range of applications available.

This ability for the average person to become a developer is also true in the robotics world. One of the tools that makes this available is Arduino, a processor board that was built to allow almost anyone to create amazing projects with little cost and even less technical expertise. This small, inexpensive, powerful board has been used in a wide range of projects. With its success, has come an entire community of developers who not only provide help in the area of software development, but also provide hardware add-ons and even new form factors for the processor board itself.

It can, however, still be a bit intimidating to start using Arduino in your projects. This book is designed to help anyone, even those with no programming background or experience, be successful in building both simple but also quite complex robotic projects. The book is designed to lead you through the process step by step so that your robotic designs can come to life.

Hopefully, this book will inspire those with the imagination and creative spirit to build those wildly inventive designs that are swirling around in their heads. One day, robots will be as pervasive as cell phones are today. So, start creating!

What this book covers

Chapter 1, *Powering on Arduino*, covers the selection of the right Arduino board for your project and how to be successful the first time you add power.

Chapter 2, *Getting Started with the Arduino IDE*, shows you how to download, install, and use the environment for your specific Arduino.

Chapter 3, Simple Programming Concepts Using the Arduino IDE, introduces basic programming constructs and how to use them within the Arduino IDE.

Chapter 4, Accessing the GPIO Pins, shows you the details of how to both send information to as well as get information from the outside world through the available GPIO capabilities.

Chapter 5, Working with Displays, shows you several different types and sizes of displays and also details how to add them to your project.

Chapter 6, Controlling DC Motors, shows you how to connect DC motors for robots that use wheels or tracks to move.

Chapter 7, Controlling Servos with Arduino, shows you how to control servos to build walking robots.

Chapter 8, Avoiding Obstacles Using Sensors, shows you how to add sensors to avoid or, perhaps, find objects.

Chapter 9, Even More Useful Sensors, shows you how to add different types of sensors to your project.

Chapter 10, Going Truly Mobile – the Remote Control of Your Robot, covers how to communicate with your robot wirelessly.

Chapter 11, Using a GPS Device with Arduino, shows you how to add a GPS device so that you always know where your robot is. This is important because if your robot gets truly mobile, it might get lost.

Chapter 12, Taking Your Robot to Sea, shows you some robots that can sail and explore under water.

Chapter 13, Robots That Can Fly, introduces you to robots that can fly.

Chapter 14, Small Projects with Arduino, shows you how to adapt other toy robots using Arduino or add a bit of flash to your current robotic projects using LEDs.

What you need for this book

The most important piece of software required for this book is the Arduino IDE, which is available at `http://www.arduino.cc/`. The only other software that will be required is the software drivers associated with the hardware that you might add to your project; these will be detailed in the individual chapters themselves.

Who this book is for

This book is for anyone with a little programming interest, a bit of imagination, and the desire to create their own amazing robotic projects. The book is designed to start by teaching beginners the basics of Arduino and programming. You'll tackle more and more challenging projects until you have the know-how to build your own complex robots that can sail, swim, and fly.

Conventions

In this book, you will find a number of styles of text that distinguish between different kinds of information. Here are some examples of these styles, and an explanation of their meaning.

Code words in text, database table names, folder names, filenames, file extensions, pathnames, dummy URLs, user input, and Twitter handles are shown as follows: "Arduino will then move to the loop() function and begin executing the statements there."

A block of code is set as follows:

```
// Pin D7 has an LED connected on FLORA.
// give it a name:
int led = 7;
// the setup routine runs once when you press RESET:
void setup() {
  // initialize the digital pin as an output.
  pinMode(led, OUTPUT);
}
// the loop routine runs over and over again forever:
void loop() {
  digitalWrite(led, HIGH);    // turn the LED on
  delay(100);                 // wait for a second
  digitalWrite(led, LOW);     // turn the LED off
  delay(1000);                // wait for a second
}
```

New terms and **important words** are shown in bold. Words that you see on the screen, in menus or dialog boxes for example, appear in the text like this: "Select the **TFTDisplayText** example by navigating to **Examples | TFT | Arduino | TFTDisplayText**."

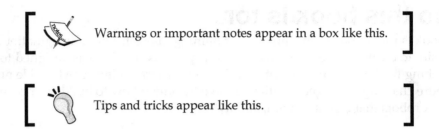

[Warnings or important notes appear in a box like this.]

[Tips and tricks appear like this.]

Reader feedback

Feedback from our readers is always welcome. Let us know what you think about this book—what you liked or may have disliked. Reader feedback is important for us to develop titles that you really get the most out of.

To send us general feedback, simply send an e-mail to feedback@packtpub.com, and mention the book title via the subject of your message.

If there is a topic that you have expertise in and you are interested in either writing or contributing to a book, see our author guide on www.packtpub.com/authors.

Customer support

Now that you are the proud owner of a Packt book, we have a number of things to help you to get the most from your purchase.

Downloading the example code

You can download the example code files for all Packt books you have purchased from your account at http://www.packtpub.com. If you purchased this book elsewhere, you can visit http://www.packtpub.com/support and register to have the files e-mailed directly to you.

Downloading the color images of this book

We also provide you a PDF file that has color images of the screenshots/diagrams used in this book. The color images will help you better understand the changes in the output. You can download this file from https://www.packtpub.com/sites/default/files/downloads/9829OS_ColoredImages.pdf.

Errata

Although we have taken every care to ensure the accuracy of our content, mistakes do happen. If you find a mistake in one of our books — maybe a mistake in the text or the code — we would be grateful if you would report this to us. By doing so, you can save other readers from frustration and help us improve subsequent versions of this book. If you find any errata, please report them by visiting `http://www.packtpub.com/submit-errata`, selecting your book, clicking on the **errata submission form** link, and entering the details of your errata. Once your errata are verified, your submission will be accepted and the errata will be uploaded on our website, or added to any list of existing errata, under the Errata section of that title. Any existing errata can be viewed by selecting your title from `http://www.packtpub.com/support`.

Piracy

Piracy of copyright material on the Internet is an ongoing problem across all media. At Packt, we take the protection of our copyright and licenses very seriously. If you come across any illegal copies of our works, in any form, on the Internet, please provide us with the location address or website name immediately so that we can pursue a remedy.

Please contact us at `copyright@packtpub.com` with a link to the suspected pirated material.

We appreciate your help in protecting our authors, and our ability to bring you valuable content.

Questions

You can contact us at `questions@packtpub.com` if you are having a problem with any aspect of the book, and we will do our best to address it.

1

Powering on Arduino

Welcome to the wonderful world of Arduino! This small but powerful processor board has become a staple with the robotic hobbyist community, and many have provided open source software to enhance its capabilities. Unfortunately, many, especially those new to embedded systems and programming, can end up so discouraged that the processor board can end up on the shelf gathering dust. The purpose of this first chapter is to help you decide which of the many different Arduinos is right for your application. Then, you'll walk through the steps to get your Arduino powered up and working so that you can begin working on all those amazing robotic projects you've always wanted to create.

Selecting the right Arduino board

Before we connect power and start programming, you'll need to decide which of the different Arduinos is right for your project.

A brief history of Arduino

First, let's understand a little history and a few definitions. Arduino began in 2005 with a few brave folks at a school in Italy deciding that providing a simple, inexpensive, easy-to-work-with **hardware** (**HW**) and **software** (**SW**) platform would be a wonderful endeavor so that their students could work on their own embedded systems projects. They started with the Atmel series of processors and then added four key elements.

First, they provided an easy-to-use hardware connection to the processor so that users didn't need to purchase expensive and difficult-to-use additional HW for this task. Initially, this connection was done via a serial port; now, it is almost universally done through USB.

Second, they provided a boot program (the program that runs when the processor powers on) that would configure the hardware and get the entire system to a known state so that users would have a standard set of hardware with which they can work. This also enables the contribution of the third key, which is the Arduino **integrated development environment** (**IDE**). It is a piece of SW that runs on a host computer and allows developers to develop their projects and then upload them easily to the target Arduino development board. The program can then be run, debugged, and modified through the IDE. Then, when the program is completed, you disconnect Arduino from the host system and it will run without any connection to the development system.

The last contribution is a set of **Input/Output** (**I/O**) pins in a standard configuration. This makes documentation easy, but more importantly, it has allowed for an entire set of additional capability to be provided by what are called shields. These shields fit on top of Arduino, plug directly into the pins, and are supported by a code library that allows the user to easily access the increased functionality.

Introducing the different versions of Arduino

Initially, there was only a single board, which made selection easy. However, as the community of Arduino users has grown, so have the many different needs for different sizes, capabilities, and form factors. There are now many different Arduino versions and even Arduino clones. There are also chips that allow you to create your very own Arduino-like systems. There are many well-known and popular versions of Arduino for you to consider for your project. However, they are too many to be listed and discussed here.

There are some that are very powerful but also have a much larger form factor and are more expensive. There are some that are extremely small and inexpensive, but they are somewhat limited in the size of programs and interfaces. Here are some of the most popular versions of Arduino.

Arduino Uno R3

Perhaps the current most popular version of Arduino is the Arduino Uno R3 (or Rev3). The following is an image of the unit:

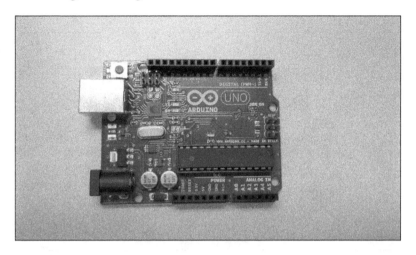

Choosing the Arduino Uno R3

This is a standard choice for many Arduino projects. It has 32 KB of space for programs, which is a relatively adequate amount for most small-to medium-size programs. It has an ATmega328 processor running at 16 MHz and the standard Arduino set of I/O pins, 14 digital I/O pins, six analog inputs, and one serial communication port. It takes a USB A Male to B Male cable, as shown in the following image:

Arduino Mega 2560 R3

Another popular choice, especially when additional program space and programming power is needed, is the Arduino Mega 2560 R3. The following is an image of this Arduino:

Choosing the Arduino Mega

The Arduino Mega is Arduino of choice for larger projects that require more programming space, a more powerful processor, more I/O, or all of these. It uses an ATmega2560 processor, which runs programs faster than the ATmega328 processor. The biggest difference, perhaps, is the larger program size. It has a total of 256 KB of memory, which can store much larger programs than the standard Arduino Uno. It also has more analog and digital I/O pins.

 The add-on shields are boards that can fit on top of Arduino to add more functionalities. However, it is important to note that they are made to fit the Arduino Uno may not fit the Arduino Mega. For each shield you are considering, make sure it will work with your particular Arduino.

Spotting a counterfeit or clone

There is one more thing to note here. Where it says Mega, you'll notice that there is no Arduino trademark on the board. The Arduino team restricts the usage of its trademark for manufacturers that pay a license fee and work with the team to ensure quality. In this case, this board is almost assuredly not an official Arduino Mega. Go to http://arduino.cc/en/Products/Counterfeit#.UxkWsfldVHI to find out more about how to spot a counterfeit.

As the hardware for Arduino is also open source, some manufacturers take this design and provide new and different designs form factors. These are considered Arduino clones. You will need to rely on the quality of the manufacturers of these clones, so consider that before purchasing.

Arduino Due

If you need even more processing speed, the most powerful of all the Arduino lines is the Arduino Due. The following is an image of this product:

Choosing the Arduino Due

The Arduino Due is truly at the top of the line as far as processing power is concerned. This unit uses the AT91SAM3X8E7 processor, which is an ARM Cortex processor. It is the same type of processor that many cell phones use. It also offers 512 KB of memory and lots of analog and digital I/O pins. Shields that are made to fit the Arduino Mega or Uno often will fit the Arduino Due, but it is always good to check before purchase. For most starter projects, you'll not need the power of the Arduino Due.

Arduino Micro

If you need to go smaller, the Arduino line also offers opportunities with much smaller packages in a number of different form factors. One of the more popular units is the Arduino Micro. The Micro is a very small form factor; yet, it has a processor with the appropriate boot parameters so that you can run the Arduino IDE, the USB connector, and the exposed I/O pins, even though they are much fewer than those found in the Arduino Uno.

The following is an image of this unit:

Choosing the Arduino Micro

This unit comes with an ATmega328 processor, the same processor that comes with the Arduino Uno, but runs at half the clock rate. It comes with the same 32 KB of memory as the Uno but with much fewer I/O pins. For this unit, and the others that I will present here, you'll need to use a mini-USB B cable, as shown in the following image:

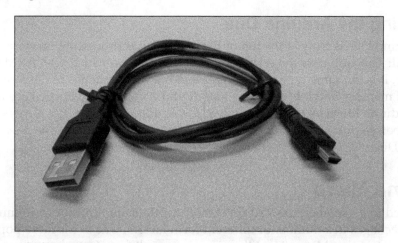

Adafruit FLORA

As noted earlier, as Arduino designs and parts are openly available, some companies have taken the standard Arduino and given it a different look. If you are looking for a much different form factor, you can try the Adafruit FLORA, offered by Adafruit at www.adafruit.com. The following is an image of this unit:

Choosing the Adafruit FLORA

The Adafruit FLORA is part of a wearable line of Arduino clone processors. It is 1.75 inches in diameter, but still has the USB connection, connectivity to the Arduino IDE, and exposed pins, but much fewer than any of the other Arduinos we have discussed. It uses the Atmega32u4 processor and also uses a mini-USB B cable.

Adafruit Gemma

If you like the FLORA form factor but want something even smaller, you can purchase the Gemma from Adafruit. In the following image, this unit is on the right-hand side of the FLORA:

Choosing the Adafruit Gemma

Amazingly, the Adafruit Gemma still has the USB connector, uses the same Arduino IDE, and has some I/O pins still available. As it has an ATtiny85 processor running at 8 MHz, only 8 KB of memory, and far fewer I/O pins, it can only be used in limited applications. However, it is an interesting form factor.

Adafruit Trinket

Finally, another small form factor Arduino from Adafruit is the Trinket. The following is an image of it with the FLORA and Gemma in the background:

Choosing the Adafruit Trinket

The trinket is very similar in performance with the Gemma, with the same processor, memory, and I/O.

Other options with Arduino

There are also other possible Arduino configurations. As you can purchase a chip that has the Arduino processor and Boot ROM configuration, you can build a custom Arduino configuration. The http://www.instructables.com/id/Paperduino-20-with-Circuit-Scribe/ website even shows you how to print your own Arduino circuit on paper.

Powering up Arduino

There is nothing as exciting as ordering and finally receiving a new piece of hardware; yet, things can go poorly even in the first few minutes. This chapter will hopefully help you avoid the pitfalls that normally accompany unpacking and configuring your Arduino. We'll step through the process, answer many of the different questions you might have, and help you understand what is going on. If you don't get through this chapter, you'll not be successful at any of the others, and your HW will go unused, which would be a real tragedy. So, let's get started.

One of the most challenging aspects of writing this guide is to decide to what level I should describe each step. Some of you are beginners, others may have some limited experience, and others will know significantly more in some of these areas. I'll try to be brief but still detail the steps to take in order to be successful.

The items you'll need for this chapter's projects are as follows:

- An Arduino
- A USB cable to go between your Arduino and the host computer
- A host computer running a Windows, Mac, or Linux operating system

Unveiling your Arduino

Before plugging anything in, inspect the board for any issues that might have occurred during shipping. This is normally not a problem, but it is always good to do a quick visual inspection. You should also acquaint yourself with the different connections on the board. In the following image, the connections on the board are labelled for your information:

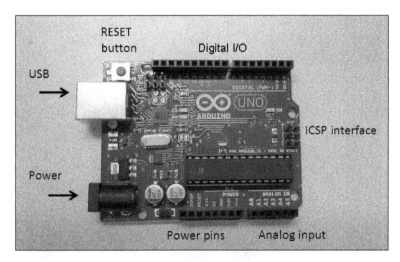

The Arduino Mega is very similar; it just has more I/O pins. However, the FLORA is a bit different. The following image shows the connections:

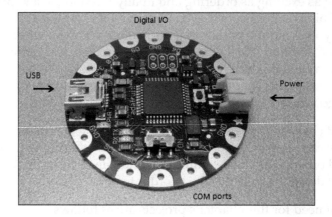

Connecting to Arduino

Before you connect the board, download the appropriate SW for your computer (Windows, Mac, or Linux from `http://arduino.cc/en/main/software#.UxoUA_ldUvs`). Install the SW by following the instructions for your board and operating system. This will also install the drivers for the board. Then, connect the board to the computer. To do this, you'll need to go through the USB-client connection. This is achieved by performing the following steps:

1. Connect the USB connector end of the cable to the board.
2. Connect the other end of the USB connector to the USB port of the PC.

When you plug the board in, the PWR LED should constantly be green. The following image shows the location of the LED so that you're certain which one to look for:

The Arduino Uno is also preloaded with a simple blink program; the yellow LED should also be turning on and off every second. The Mega will look very similar to the Arduino Uno.

Installing the FLORA IDE

If you are using the FLORA Arduino, you should get your Arduino IDE from `http://learn.adafruit.com/getting-started-with-flora/download-software`. Unzip the file and place it in a directory where you can get to it later. Then, use the USB cable to connect the device to the computer. When the device is connected, it should look like the following image when powered on:

Don't worry yet about the blinking red LED; I'll explain this in *Chapter 2, Getting Started with the Arduino IDE*.

Summary

Congratulations! You've completed the first stage of your journey. If you haven't purchased your Arduino yet, feel free to go out and start your Arduino experience. If you have, you should have your Arduino up and working. No gathering dust in the bin for this piece of hardware. It is now ready to start connecting to all sorts of interesting devices in all sorts of interesting ways.

Your system has lots of capabilities. Your next step will be learning how to bring up the Arduino IDE so that you can start doing all sorts of amazing things with your Arduino.

2

Getting Started with the Arduino IDE

Now that you have Arduino connected to power, you are ready to start the IDE. In this chapter, I'll start by covering how to use the IDE in Windows. Then, I'll cover any specific change you might need to make if you are using a Mac.

For this chapter, the objectives are as follows:

- Load and configure the Arduino IDE
- Download and run a simple example program

As discussed previously, Arduino comes in many flavors and there are too many to include an example for each one. Sometimes, individual boards will need a special version of the IDE. This book will focus primarily on Uno, perhaps the most popular of Arduino variants. Here and there I'll also throw in an example or two from Mega and one of the small Arduino form factors, FLORA. There are two versions of the IDE: 1.0.x and 1.5.x. Most of your work will be done with 1.0.x, but I'll show you when to use 1.5.x for some newer versions of Arduino. You don't need a board to experiment with the IDE, but it will make much more sense if you have one.

Using a Windows machine to develop with Arduino

If you are using a newer version of Microsoft Windows and the Arduino Uno, when you plug Arduino into the system, it will automatically try to install the drivers. If the device fails to install, you may have to tell it where the drivers are. You will know when this happens — you will be prompted with an error message saying **Device driver software was not successfully installed**. If you get this error, follow the directions at `http://Arduino.cc/en/Guide/Windows#.UxoWXPldUvt`.

When your drivers are installed, you should see the following device when you navigate to **Start Menu | Devices and Printers**:

In this case, the device is connected to COM port 23. Note down the COM port Arduino is connected to as you'll need that in a minute. If you are using an Apple Mac or Linux machine, follow the instructions at arduino.cc/en/Guide/MacOSX for Mac and playground.arduino.cc/Learning/Linux for Linux on how to determine your USB port connection.

Running the IDE for Uno

Now that the device is installed, you can run the IDE. Select the IDE icon that should have been installed on the desktop as shown in the following screenshot:

When you select this icon, the IDE should start and you should see something like the following screenshot:

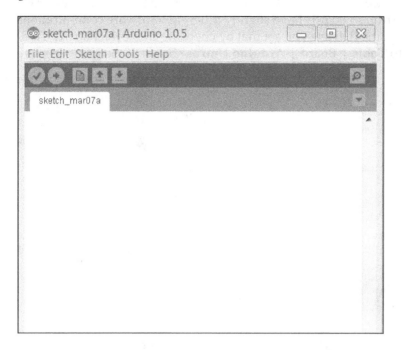

This is the environment you will use to develop your applications. The IDE will then make it easy to compile the code, upload it to the device, and run it.

Setting the IDE to your board

First, you'll need to set the IDE to create code for the proper processor because different Arduino boards have slightly different hardware configurations. Fortunately, the IDE lets you set that by choosing the correct board. To do this, navigate to **Tools | Board | Arduino Uno** as shown in the following screenshot:

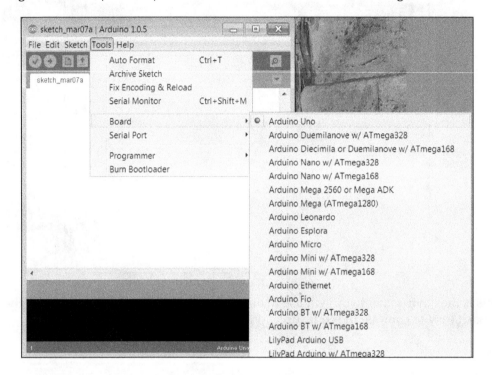

Selecting the proper COM port

The next step is to select the proper COM port. To do this, navigate to **Tools | Serial Port | COM23** (the port you noted earlier), as shown in the following screenshot:

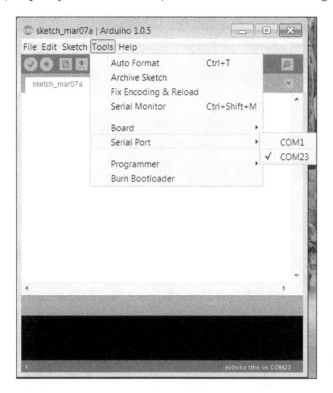

The IDE should now indicate that you are using the Arduino Uno on COM23 in the lower-right corner of the IDE, as seen in the preceding screenshot.

Opening and uploading a file to Arduino

Now you can open and upload a simple example file. It is called the Blink application. It has already been written for you, so you won't need to do any coding.

To get a Blink application, perform the following steps:

1. Navigate to **File | Examples | 01.Basics | Blink** as shown in the following screenshot:

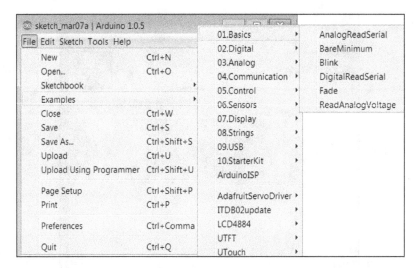

2. You should then see the Blink code in the IDE window:

3. Select the **Upload** button as shown in the following screenshot:

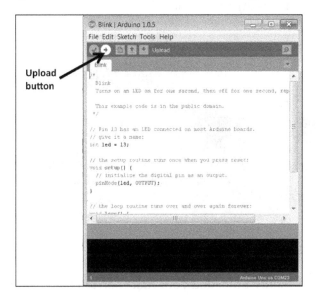

4. Once you have uploaded the file, it will give you an indication in the lower-left corner of the IDE display that the file has been uploaded:

5. When the program is uploaded, it will automatically start running and the orange LED on the Arduino Uno will blink:

You have now successfully uploaded your first code to your Arduino!

Running the IDE for Mega

If you are using Mega, it will be very similar. Connecting the unit via USB and then navigating to **Start Menu | Devices and Printers** will show the following device:

Note that in this case, Mega is connected to COM port 24. The port that Arduino will be connected to is selected by the computer and is not the same for all Arduinos. The only difference between the instructions for using Mega and Uno is that you will need to set the correct board type for Mega. To do this, navigate to **Tools | Board | Arduino Mega 2560 or Mega ADK** as shown in the following screenshot:

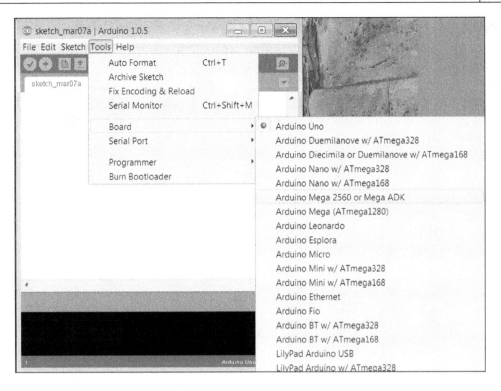

If you have a different COM port number, make sure you set that by navigating to **Tools | Serial Port.** You can now upload the Blink code, and the orange LED should be blinking on Mega.

Running the IDE for the Adafruit FLORA

When connecting the FLORA device, you'll need to have the Adafruit version of the IDE installed. You can download this from `learn.adafruit.com/getting-started-with-flora/download-software`. Follow the directions on this site to download and install the IDE. Since the FLORA device is not standard Arduino, this will add another selection to the **Board** type for the Arduino IDE.

Installing the Adafruit drivers

When plugging in the device, if it fails to install, you may have to tell it where to find the drivers. You will know if this happens—you will get an error message saying **Device driver software was not successfully installed**. If you get this error, follow the directions at `http://Arduino.cc/en/Guide/Windows#.UxoWXPldUvt`; only point your driver to the directory from where you downloaded the Adafruit IDE. For example, in my case, I am running 64 bit Windows, so I will select **windows** as shown in the following screenshot:

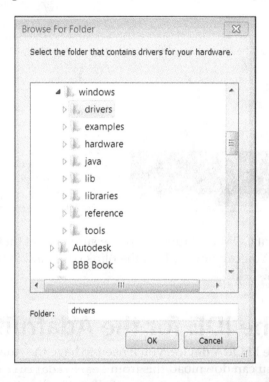

It will probably complain about an unsigned driver, but accept the driver anyway. In the end, you should be able to see the FLORA device when you navigate to **Start Menu | Devices and Printers** as shown in the following screenshot:

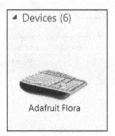

When you select this device and look at its properties, you should see something like the following screenshot:

Note the device COM port; in this case, it is COM25. Now, you should open the Adafruit Arduino IDE by going to the directory where you unzipped the files and select the Arduino IDE. Just a note, since I often use both types of Arduino devices, I have a separate directory for the standard Arduino IDE and a different location for the Adafruit Arduino IDE. To open the Adafruit Arduino IDE, I go to the file browser and select the Arduino IDE executable:

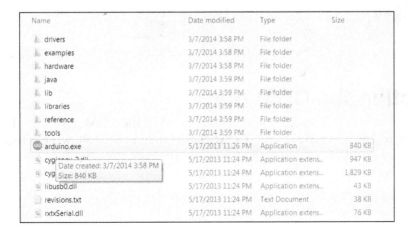

Selecting the Adafruit boards

The Arduino IDE should start and look very much like it did for Arduino Uno or Mega. However, when you select board by going to **Tools | Board**, you should see four new selections at the bottom:

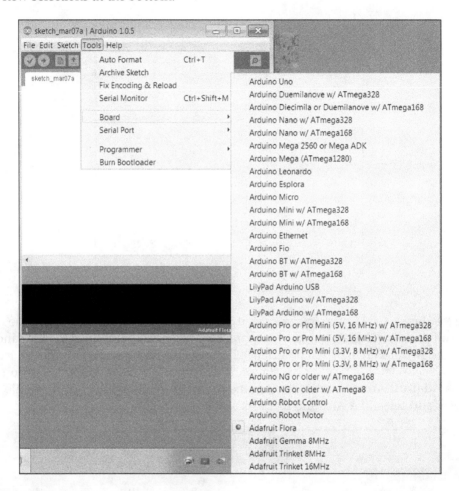

Selecting the COM port

Now that your board is selected, you'll need to select the COM port. Do this by navigating to **Tools | Serial Port | COM25** as shown in the following screenshot:

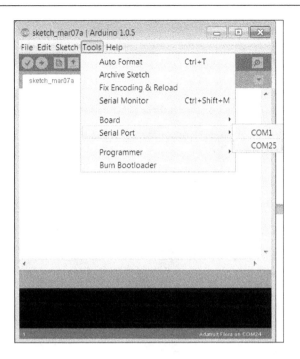

Coding an LED flash on the FLORA

Now you should be able to upload a file. You can't use the earlier Blink example as we don't have the same I/O pins. So, type the following code into the IDE interface:

```
// Pin D7 has an LED connected on FLORA.
// give it a name:
int led = 7;
// the setup routine runs once when you press RESET:
void setup() {
  // initialize the digital pin as an output.
  pinMode(led, OUTPUT);
}
// the loop routine runs over and over again forever:
void loop() {
  digitalWrite(led, HIGH);   // turn the LED on
  delay(100);                // wait for a second
  digitalWrite(led, LOW);    // turn the LED off
  delay(1000);               // wait for a second
}
```

Downloading the example code

You can download the example code files for all the Packt books you have purchased from your account at http://www.packtpub.com. If you purchased this book elsewhere, you can visit http://www.packtpub.com/support and register to have the files e-mailed to you.

Don't worry about specific code details yet, but this code will flash the LED on FLORA. Upload the code by clicking on the **Upload** button as follows:

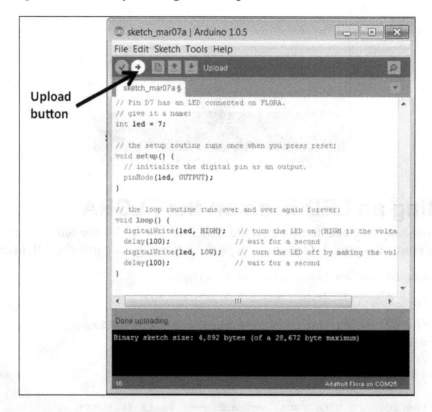

When you have uploaded the file, you should get an indication in the lower-left corner of the IDE. Now the red LED should be flashing much faster. You can change the delay(1000) value and see different flash timing.

Using a Mac to develop using Arduino

Using a Mac or a Windows machine is absolutely fine; however, you'll just need to follow a couple of different steps. First, as noted earlier, download and install the Mac software from `http://Arduino.cc/en/guide/macOSX#.UxpobfldVHI`. When you plug in your Arduino Uno or Mega, the system will recognize it and establish a connection. The green power LED should turn on. Now, open the Arduino IDE and select the proper board as shown previously.

You will also need to select the serial port. When you navigate to the **Tools | Serial Port**, you should see the following screenshot:

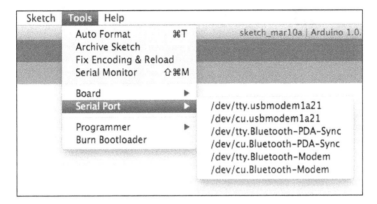

Select the option that begins with **tty.usbmodem**. You may need to remove Arduino to see if you have other devices connected to the port and how this selection changes to identify which port is connected to Arduino. You'll then be connected to the device. You should now be able to open the Blink example, run the code, and see the orange LED flash.

If you are using FLORA, Gemma, or Trinket, you'll need to go to `https://learn. adafruit.com/getting-started-with-flora/download-software` and follow the instructions to download and install the SW. Then, go to **Tools | Serial Port** as shown earlier for Arduino Uno and Mega.

Summary

You've completed the next stage of your journey. You have your Arduino up and talking to your external computer and you know how to connect to the IDE to develop code. Your next step will be to learn some programming basics so that you can start doing all sorts of amazing things with your Arduino. You'll be able to build robots that can move and sense their environment.

3
Simple Programming Concepts Using the Arduino IDE

Now that you have downloaded, installed, and initiated the Arduino IDE, in this chapter, you'll learn some basic programming concepts. If you are already comfortable with programming, especially the C programming language, you can skip this chapter. If you're not, or need a quick review, this chapter discusses some simple programming examples on how to program Arduino. At the end of the chapter, I'll cover additional important programming constructs.

To get started, open your Arduino IDE and make sure your Arduino is connected to your development environment via its USB cable. You may want to open and run the Blink example from *Chapter 2, Getting Started with the Arduino IDE*. When you have uploaded the file successfully, the IDE should tell you by displaying **Done uploading** in the lower-left corner of the IDE.

The program should also be running on Arduino and the orange LED blinking. If all of this seems clear and natural, you may consider skipping this chapter. If, however, this all feels new to you, welcome to *Chapter 3, Simple Programming Concepts Using the Arduino IDE*! In this chapter, you'll learn about creating, editing, and running programs on Arduino.

Creating, editing, and saving files on Arduino

You know how to start the IDE, but you've not been introduced to all the available functionalities. So let's take a quick tour of the IDE. Again, here is what the IDE should look like when you first start it up:

Note that at the top of the IDE, there are five topic menus: **File**, **Edit**, **Sketch**, **Tools**, and **Help**. Each of these tabs holds a set of functionalities that you'll need. If you select the **File** tab, you should see the following screenshot:

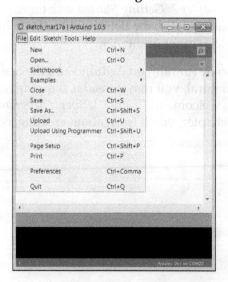

These selections let you create, open, upload, and print files in the Arduino IDE. Once you click on **File**, you will get the following options:

- **New**: This is straightforward; you use this if you want to create a new file.

- **Open...**: This is equally clear; select this if you want to open a file that you created earlier.

- **Sketchbook**: This is probably a new term, one with which you are not familiar. Arduino programs are called sketches, and **Sketchbook** keeps track of sketches you have created. You'll also find sketches placed there if you have downloaded libraries associated with additional HW shields you may have purchased.

- **Examples**: This selection has a treasure trove of example programs created by the Arduino community. The IDE comes with a number of basic examples, but as an additional functionality associated with HW, others can place examples there as well. *Chapter 4*, *Accessing the GPIO Pins*, will cover this in more detail.

- **Close**: This is self-explanatory; it will close the open sketch.

- **Save** and **Save As...**: These allow you to save a sketch to a file. Generally, these will be appended with the .ino extension to differentiate them from other files.

- **Upload**: You've already used the **Upload** menu; it has the same function as clicking the **Upload** button directly on the IDE. This will compile and send your code to your Arduino.

- **Upload Using Programmer**: This is used only when you want an external programmer to upload code to Arduino. This is sometimes used when you have access to an external programmer and don't want to use the Arduino bootloader. To know more about this case, visit http://Arduino.cc/en/ Hacking/Programmer#.Uyhr_IUXdNp.

- **Page Setup** and **Print**: These allow you to set up and print your sketch.

- **Preferences**: This brings up a set of selections to set defaults, including where to store your sketches, the default language, and other settings that you normally don't need to change.

If you click on the **Edit** tab, you will see the following options:

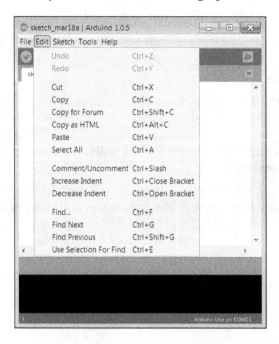

I'll not cover each of these options in detail; they are standard edit-type commands. If you click on the **Sketch** tab, you should see the following screenshot:

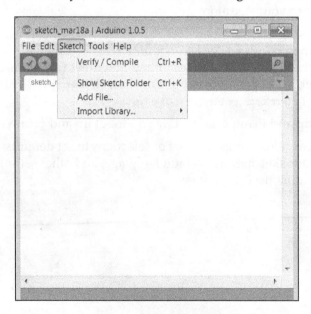

Under the **Sketch** tab, you will get the following options:

- **Verify / Compile**: This allows you to compile and verify your code. This checks whether your code can actually be turned into a program that can be run on Arduino before you try and upload it to the hardware.

- **Show Sketch Folder**: This will open a window that shows all of the sketches in the default directory.

- **Add File…**: This allows you to add a file to your sketch. Now that may seem odd because you may have assumed that a sketch is a file. But a sketch can contain code that is not just in one file but in several files. We will cover this feature later in the chapter.

- **Import Library…**: This is an important option as it allows you to bring in code capabilities that someone else developed; often this is associated with additional hardware that you want to access. Arduino already comes with a large number of functions that you have access to. You don't have to write these sets of code because they are available for you to simply call. You can also add to this set of functionalities by importing additional libraries. Additional HW normally comes with code libraries that provide access to its features. Instead of having to cut and paste this code into your code window or add the files to your sketch, importing these files as libraries allows you to access the functionalities as if they were in files already associated with your sketch.

The next menu is the **Tools** tab. When you click on it, you should see the following screenshot:

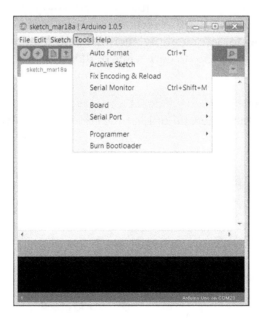

You've already used the **Board** and **Serial Port** selections. The other choices under the **Tools** tab are as follows:

- **Auto Format**: This automatically formats the code in the current sketch, placing indents where it thinks they should be.

- **Archive Sketch**: This takes the sketch and file associated with it and places them in a *.zip file in the same directory.

- **Fix Encoding & Reload**: This will sometimes clean up files that are encoded with characters that can't be displayed correctly.

- **Serial Monitor**: This opens a serial connection between you and Arduino. You can use this to communicate with the board via a USB connection that acts like a serial port. You'll need to have the serial communication commands in your code.

- **Programmer** and **Burn Bootloader**: These allow you to access an Arduino system without the bootloader. However, since you won't be requiring these, we'll not cover them here.

The last menu, **Help**, provides help selections. It's simple and self-explanatory, so you can explore the help system on your own. Now that you know your way around the IDE, you can start programming your Arduino.

Basic C programming on Arduino

In this section, you'll learn about the C programming language, the language supported by the Arduino IDE. In this section, we are going to cover some basic concepts. If you are new to programming, there are a number of different websites that provide tutorials. If you'd like to practice some of the basic programming concepts in C, try www.cprogramming.com/tutorial.html or http://www.learn-c.org/.

In this section, we'll cover how to create a basic sketch. We'll also cover how to enter some C code, compile the code, and upload the code to your Arduino.

To open a new sketch from the IDE that contains the minimum basic code, navigate to **File | Examples | 01.Basics | BareMinimum**. You should now see this in your sketch as shown in the following screenshot:

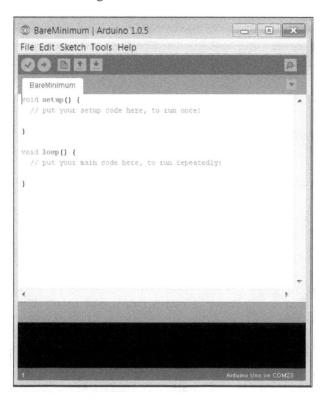

This basic sketch provides two functions; a function is simply an organized set of instructions that Arduino will execute. When Arduino is powered on, it begins to execute a list of instructions one by one. These start in the bootloader that configures everything and gets Arduino to a state that you can use it. Once Arduino has completed executing the bootloader, it looks for the setup() function. In this function, you will specify any additional setup activity that you need Arduino to do. Arduino will then move to the loop() function and begin executing the statements there. This loop() function will be run not once, but over and over again until the power is turned off.

Now that you have context, you can actually start writing some code in the setup() and loop() functions. Start by putting something in the setup() function. Change the setup() function to look like the code in the following screenshot:

There are two changes that should have been made. The first change is adding the int led = 13; statement. This statement sets up a storage location in the memory named led and puts the value 13 into this variable. Since this variable is declared outside of any function, it is a global variable. Global variables are available to all functions. This particular variable will hold the value of the output pin that will light up your LED. Note that you need to declare the type of variable that tells Arduino how big a storage location to set aside for the variable. There are many types available but you'll use just a few; int for the value that has no decimal, float for values that have a decimal, char for character variables, and bool for values that are just true or false. The second change is adding the pinMode(led, OUTPUT); statement. This statement calls the pinMode function and passes led and OUTPUT to the values in the function's argument.

Now you might be a bit confused because the `pinMode(led, OUTPUT)` function is nowhere to be found in your code. This is a library function provided by the Arduino system. This particular function takes two arguments: the value of the pin to be set and the `INPUT` or `OUTPUT` state. In this case, you want pin 13 (the value stored in LED) to be an OUTPUT. The GPIO pin on Arduino can be configured as input or output, that is, they can either accept or send a signal.

Now you can compile and verify your code. However, save your code under the file name first. To do this, click on **File** and then click on **Save As...**. This will open a dialog window, enter first, and then click on **Save**. Your IDE should now look something like this:

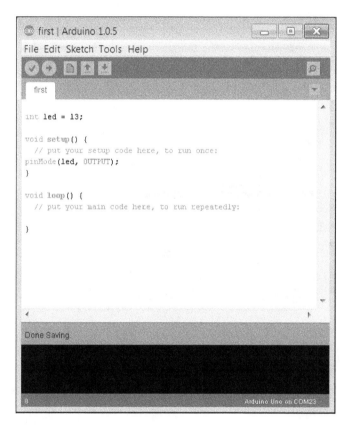

Now compile and verify your code, just to make sure you've typed in everything correctly. To do this, navigate to **Sketch | Verify / Compile**, as shown in the following screenshot:

You should see something like this:

When the compile is complete, you should see something like the following screenshot:

You could also upload and run your program, but it won't do anything yet, as you have not added enough functionality. You've only defined pin 13 (the one connected to the LED) as OUTPUT. To actually see something on your Arduino, you'll need to add some code to the loop() function. Now add the code shown in the following screenshot to the loop() function:

You have added the `digitalWrite(led, HIGH);` statement to your loop. This is another function that is available from the standard Arduino library. This will, each time through the loop, tell the pin 13 (defined with the `pinMode(led, OUTPUT);` statement) to go high or low. Save your file, and this time you can compile and upload your code by navigating to **File | Upload**. You can also use the **Upload** button.

This selection will compile your code and upload it to Arduino. If everything went as it should, your Arduino's orange LED should be solidly lit. Now, you can add a bit more code to make it blink. Change your code and add the following lines of code to the `loop()` function:

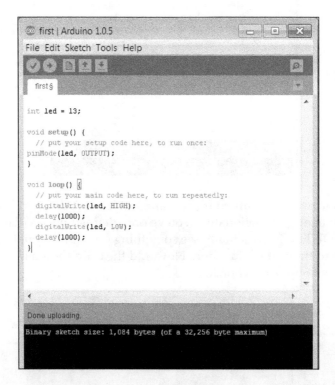

The `delay(1000);` function is another function that is provided by the standard Arduino library and this pauses the program for 1000 msec (there are a 1000 msec in a second). The `digitalWrite(led, LOW);` function then writes a 0 to the output pin, which should turn the LED off. The `delay(1000);` function pauses the program again. The 1000 in the parentheses is an excellent example of an argument that you pass to a function. In this case, each time you call the `delay()` function you send it a number that tells it how long to pause. This `loop()` function will be called continually, so this should turn the LED on and off. Upload this code as you did the last time, and you will now see the orange LED flash on and off.

It might be helpful to show you what happens when you make a mistake. If I type `LO` instead of `LOW` in the second `digitalWrite(led, LO);` function and tried the upload, I would see something like the following screenshot:

Note that the yellow band shows me the line I mistyped, and tells me: **'LO' was not declared in this scope**. Misspellings are one of the biggest reasons why your code might not compile, so check your spellings when you see something like this.

You now know the details behind your first sketch! Play with different values of the argument in the `delay(1000)` function, and your LED should flash at different rates.

Basic programming constructs on Arduino

Now that you know how to enter and run a simple C program on Arduino, let's look at some additional programming constructs. Specifically, you'll see what to do when you want to decide between two instructions to execute and how to execute a set of instructions a number of times.

The if statement

As you have seen, your programs normally start with the first line of code and then continue executing the next line until your program runs out of code. This is fine, but what if you want to decide between two different courses of action? We can do this in C using an `if` statement. The following screenshot shows some example code:

You'll need to make several changes this time. The first is to add another global variable, `int whichLED = 1;` at the top of your program. Then, you'll need to add several statements to your `loop()` function. The line-by-line details are as follows:

- `if (whichLED == 1):` This is the `if` statement. The `if` statement evaluates the expression inside the parentheses. This is the check statement. If it is true, it executes the next statement or a set of statements enclosed by { }. Note that we use the `==` operator instead of a single `=` operator. A single `=` operator in C is the assignment operator, which means the storage location on the right is assigned the value on the left. The `==` operator is a comparison operator, and returns true if the two values are equal and false if they are not.

- `{:` This begins the set of statements the program will execute if the comparison statement is true.

- `digitalWrite(led, HIGH);:` The four statements that turn the LED on and off at a 100 msec rate are `delay(100);`, `digitalWrite(led, LOW);`, `delay(100);`, and `whichLED = 0;`.The `whichLED` variable is assigned a value of 0. This will make sure the next time through the loop it will execute the else statement.

- `}:` This ends the set of statements that will be executed if the comparison statement is true.

- `else:` This statement, which is optional, defines a statement or set of statements that should be executed if the comparison statement is false.

- `{:` This begins the set of statements the program will execute if the comparison statement returns false.

- `digitalWrite(led, HIGH);:` The four statements that turn the LED on and off at a 1000 msec rate are `delay(1000);`, `digitalWrite(led, LOW);`, `delay(1000);`, and `whichLED=1;`. The `whichLED` variable is assigned a value of 1. This will make sure that next time it will execute the if statement through the loop.

When you have this code typed in, you can upload it. When it is uploaded, you should see a short flash of the LED, followed by a longer flash, much like a heartbeat.

The for statement

Another useful construct is the `for` construct; it will allow us to execute a set of statements over and over for a specific number of times. The following screenshot shows an example using this construct:

The code in the preceding screenshot looks very similar to the code you've used before, but we've added two examples of the `for` construct. Some details of the `loop()` function are as follows:

- `for (int i = 0; i < 5; i++)`: This loop consists of three elements. The `int i = 0;` is the initializer statement. It is only done once when you first execute the loop. In this case, the initializer statement creates a storage location named `i` and puts the value of `0` in it. The second part of the loop statement is the check statement. In this case, the check statement is `i < 5`. If the statement is true, the loop executes. If it is false, the loop stops and the program goes to the next statement after the `for` loop. The final part of the `for` loop is a statement that is executed at the end of each loop. In this case, the statement `i++` simply means the processor will add one to the `i` value at the end of each loop. This will be looped five times for `i` equals to 0, 1, 2, 3, and 4. The check statement will fail when `i` equals 5 and the loop will stop.

- `{`: This bracket defines the start of the statements that may be looped.

- `digitalWrite(led, HIGH);`: The statements that will be executed each time through the loop and flash the LED light quickly are `delay(100);`, `digitalWrite(led, LOW);`, and `delay(100);`.

- `}`: This ends the loop. When this statement is reached each time through the loop, the loop statement is executed and the execution goes back to the top of the loop, where the check statement is evaluated. If it is true, the statement is executed again. If it is false, the loop stops and the statement following the loop is executed.

- `for (int i = 0; i < 5; i++)`: This is another loop, just like the previous one, except it flashes the LED for a long time. Just like the first loop, it is executed five times.

- `{`: This bracket defines the start of the statements that may be looped.

- `digitalWrite(led, HIGH);`: The statements that will be executed each time through the loop and will flash the LED light quickly are `delay(1000);`, `digitalWrite(led, LOW);`, and `delay(1000);`.

- `}`: This ends the loop.

Now you can upload the program and see that there are five long flashes of the orange LED followed by five short flashes.

Summary

In this chapter, you've learned how to interact with the Arduino IDE and create, edit, upload, and run programs on Arduino. You have also been exposed to the C programming language. If this is your first experience with programming, don't be surprised if you are still uneasy with programing in general and the if and for statements in particular. You probably felt just as uncomfortable with your first introduction to the English language; you just may not remember it.

It is always a bit difficult to try new things. However, I will try to give you explicit instructions on what to type so that you can be successful. There is one major challenge when working with computers. They always do exactly what you tell them to do and not necessarily what you want them to do. So, if you encounter problems, check several times to make sure that your code matches the example exactly. In the next chapter, you'll learn to access the GPIO pins to interface with the outside world.

4
Accessing the GPIO Pins

Now that you are familiar with the Arduino IDE and how to create, edit, and upload a program, this chapter will now turn your focus to the HW. You'll get a chance to learn how to connect to and access the capabilities of the **general purpose input/output (GPIO)** pins from the SW. In this chapter, I'll start by explaining the GPIO pins, what they can and can't do, and then show you how to make Arduino access the outside world with the help of some very basic circuits and very simple programming examples.

The GPIO capability of Arduino

Arduino was built to access the outside world. Much of that access is through the GPIO pins. Each Arduino board has a different set of GPIO pins, so in this section, I'll provide details on the GPIO pins available on the most common variant of Arduino: Arduino Uno. Then, I'll also document the additional capability of the Arduino Mega. Finally, I'll show the GPIO capability of a more limited Arduino: Arduino FLORA.

First, let's focus on the Arduino Uno. As described in *Chapter 1, Powering on Arduino*, the Arduino Uno comes with a set of 14 digital and six analog I/O pins, along with some additional pins to provide power and serial I/O.

Fortunately, the pins are actually well labeled on the board itself, as shown in the following image:

The following table shows a list of pins that are available and a brief description of what each pin can do, starting at the upper-right side of the board and going clockwise. A more in-depth description of these pins will come later as you actually use them in some example projects:

Arduino Pin	Description
AREF	This pin provides a reference voltage for the analog inputs. The values on the analog pins will be reported in reference to this voltage. You'll also use this in some applications to provide a reference voltage for some sensing devices. You can also provide an external reference value to this pin, which means that the numerical values of the inputs will be scaled according to the value supplied on this pin.
GND	This pin provides a ground reference for the AREF pin.
Digital ((PWM~) 13/2	These 11 pins can be used to either read or write digital values. If defined as an input, the value will be read as either 0 or 1 based on the voltage level at the input. If defined as an output, the value will be set to either a 0 or 1 logic voltage level. (The actual voltage will depend on the voltage logic level of your Arduino. Some are 5 V logic level, while others are 3.3 V logic level.)
Digital TX->1	This pin and the RX pin next to it provide a serial interface that can be used to communicate with other devices.
Digital RX->0	This pin and the TX pin next to it provide a serial interface that can be used to communicate with other devices.

Arduino Pin	Description
Analog IN A5/A0	These pins do double duty. Normally, they would be used as A/D inputs to Arduino to read continuous voltage values and turn them into integer values. However, they can also be used as digital I/O, very similar to the digital I/O pins.
Power Vin	You can power your Arduino from this pin. This can be especially useful after you have uploaded your program; you can then disconnect the USB port, and when you apply voltage to this pin, your Arduino will boot and run the uploaded program. You can use a voltage value from 7 to 12 volts, so a wide variety of DC power adapters or battery configurations can be used.
Power GND	This pin is the ground connection associated with the Power Vin connection.
Power GND	This is a ground connection normally associated with the Power 5 V and Power 3.3 V outputs.
Power 5 V	This is a voltage output set to 5 V.
Power 3.3 V	This is a voltage output set to 3.3 V.
RESET	This pin will reset the processor, which will cause the program to be run from the beginning.
IOREF	This provides either a 3.3 V or 5 V reference, indicating the logic level of the board.

The Mega provides a bit more from an I/O pin perspective. The following image shows the Arduino board:

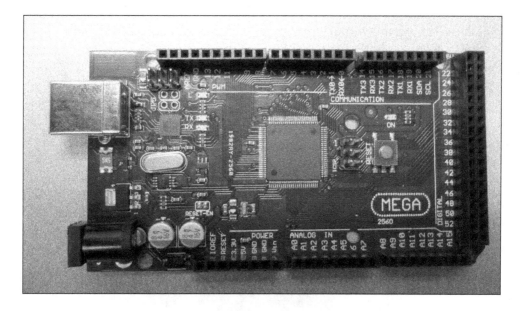

You'll first notice that the pins on the left side of the Arduino Mega are labeled the same as with the Arduino Uno. And they do have the same functionality. However, you'll also notice some additional pins on the right side of the board. The following table provides a brief explanation of the most useful pins, starting at the upper-right side of the board and going clockwise:

Arduino Mega pin	Description
Communication TX3/RX3/ TX2/RX2/TX1/RX1	These pins add three more serial I/O ports. Mega supports four serial I/O ports.
SDA/SDL	These pins support the I2C I/O port. This is a special purpose communication that supports addressing, so you can talk to more than one device.
Digital I/O pins 44-46	Additional digital I/O pins that can be used to either read or write digital values. If input, the value will be read as either a 0 or 1 based on the voltage level at the input. If output, the value will be set to either a 0 or 1 logic voltage level. (The actual voltage will depend on the voltage logic level of your Arduino. Some are 5 V logic level, while others are 3.3 V logic level.)
Digital 50-53	These pins provide an SPI interface, particularly useful for video.
Analog In 6-15	These are additional analog DSP inputs that operate the same as the A0 to A6 pins.

The FLORA, being a much smaller package, provides a different set of pins. The following image shows the FLORA:

The following table gives a description of the pins available, starting at the upper-left side of the board just above the USB connector:

Arduino FLORA pin	Description
3.3 V	This is a voltage output set to 3.3 volts. There are two of these pins available on the Arduino FLORA.
Digital I/O pins D10, D9, D6, D12	These pins can be used to either read or write digital values. If defined as an input, the value will be read as either a 0 or 1 based on the voltage level at the input. If defined as an output, the value will be set to either a 0 or 1 logic voltage level. The FLORA uses 3.3 V for 1 and 0 V for 0.
GND	There are three GND pins on the FLORA. The one closest to the white battery connector (the connector opposite the USB port) is normally used as the ground connection from the battery. The other two GND pins can be used for the digital I/O pins or the 3.3 V outputs.
VBATT	You can power the Arduino FLORA from this pin. This can be especially useful after you have uploaded your program; you can then disconnect the USB port, and when you apply voltage to this pin, your Arduino FLORA will boot and run the uploaded program. You can use a voltage value from 7 to 16 volts, so a wide variety of DC power adapters or battery configurations can be used.
Digital TX->1	This pin, and the RX pin next to it, provide a serial interface that can be used to communicate with other devices.
Digital RX->0	This pin, and the TX pin next to it, provide a serial interface that can be used to communicate with other devices.
SDA/SDL	These pins support the I2C I/O port. This is a special purpose communication that supports addressing, so you can talk to more than one device.

The first external hardware connection

Now that you are aware of all of the GPIO capabilities, you can start putting them to work. In order to do this, it is best to purchase a small breadboard and some jumper wires; this will make connecting to the outside world easier.

They are easy to find. You can purchase one at almost any electronics store or on any online electronics site. The jumper wires you want are male-to-male solderless jumper wires.

 These jumper cables plug easily into the header pins on the Arduino Uno or Mega and the breadboard. If you are working with FLORA, you will want to purchase some alligator clip style wires. These will make connecting to FLORA easy.

There are also many starter kits which come with breadboards and jumper cables, along with additional sensors and HW capabilities that you can use with your Arduino board. There are too many to list here; simply search Arduino starter kits on the Internet and you'll get an idea of the many choices. Just make sure they come with a breadboard and male-to-male solderless jumper wires.

Your first project will use the digital I/O pins to light up an LED. To do this, you'll need to gather two more hardware pieces. The first is a **light emitting diode** (**LED**). This is a small part with two leads that lights up when voltage is applied to it. They come in a wide variety of colors. If you want to buy them online, search for a 3 mm LED. You can also get them at most electronics shops.

You'll also need a resistor to limit the current to the LED; a 220 ohm resister would be the right size. Again, you can get them online or at most electronics shops.

If you get three LEDs and three resistors, you can exercise several of the digital I/O pins.

Now that you have all the bits and bobs, let's build our first hardware project. Before you plug anything in, let's look at the breadboard for a moment so that you can understand how you are going to use it to make connections. You'll be plugging your wires into the holes on the breadboard. The holes on the breadboard are connected in a unique way to make the connections you desire.

In the middle of the board, the holes are connected across the board. So, if you plug in a wire, and another wire in the hole right next to it, these two wires will be connected, as shown in the following image:

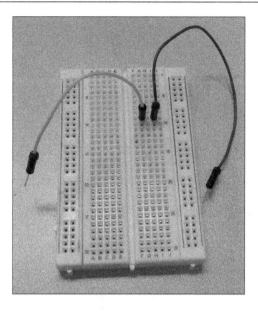

 The two rows on each side of the board are generally designed to provide power, so they are connected up and down.

So, let's place the electronic parts on the breadboard. Place the LEDs so that one wire is on one side of the middle split of the breadboard. The direction of the LED is important; make sure the longer of the two wires is on the left side of the hole.

Now, place the resisters on the holes on one side. The direction of the resistor does not make any difference, but make sure the second wire lead is placed in the row of holes at the end of the board.

These will all be connected together, and will be connected to the GND of your Arduino using one of the jumper cables, as shown in the following image:

Finally, use jumper wires to connect the digital I/O pins 13, 12, and 11 to the holes on the breadboard, as shown in the following image:

Now that the HW is configured correctly, you'll need to add code to activate the LEDs.

The Arduino IDE and LED code

To create the LED code, start the Arduino IDE. Then, recall the code you wrote in *Chapter 1, Powering on Arduino*. The IDE should look like the following screenshot:

In this code, setting led 13 lit the orange LED on the board. It turns out that the led output pin 13 is also the connection to pin 13 on the connector of the Arduino Uno. If you upload and run this program, the LED connected to pin 13 should flash at the same rate as the LED on the Arduino Uno, as shown in the following image:

You'll need to add a similar bit of code to get the LEDs connected to pins 12 and 11. Add the code snippet that can be seen in the following screenshot to the sketch on the Arduino IDE:

Here, you are replicating the code for the `led` connected to pin 13 to the second `led1` connected to pin 12 and the third `led2` connected to pin 13. You then program them all to be output pins, and then in the main loop, toggle between high and low. Note that I have two toggling together (pins 13 and 11) with the other (pin 12) toggling in the exact opposite sequence. First, the two outer LEDs should light for one second, and then the inner LED should light.

If one or more of the LEDs don't light, check to make sure that they are pushed firmly down into the board. You can also change the direction of the LED; perhaps you have the leads in the wrong direction on the board.

You can do the same thing with the FLORA board, but you'll need to use alligator clips to connect from FLORA to the breadboard. To do this, build the breadboard as shown earlier. Then, connect the first alligator clip to the right side of one of the resistors on the breadboard. After this, connect it to the GND connector on FLORA. Then, connect the alligator clips to LED 10 and the left side of the top of the breadboard.

Once you have done that, connect the other two LEDs to the LED 12 and LED 9 pins, as shown in the following image:

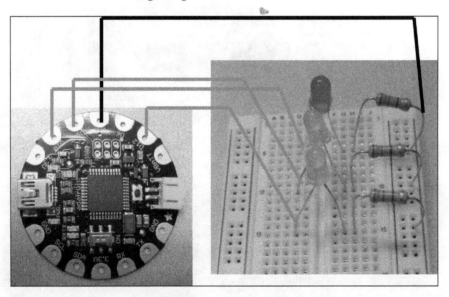

Now, bring up the Arduino IDE associated with FLORA. Create the code shown in the following screenshot, patterned after the code you created in *Chapter 1, Powering on Arduino*:

In this case, you are going to use D12, D10, and D9 to flash the LEDs on the breadboard. On the IDE, make sure that Adafruit FLORA is set up on the correct COM port. Upload the code and you should see your flashing LEDs.

Summary

That's it! You've completed your very first hardware project. You can play with different patterns of LED sequences by using for loops and different wait states. Now that you have created your very first HW project, in the next chapter, we'll cover how to add HW capabilities using an HW shield, a piece of HW that plugs directly into the I/O connectors of your Arduino.

5
Working with Displays

In *Chapter 4*, *Accessing the GPIO Pins*, you learned how to connect with the outside world using jumper wires, breadboards, and components. In this chapter, you'll learn different connection approaches to show how you can connect an additional capability to Arduino using hardware shields designed for Arduino. Specifically, I'll cover two topics: how to add a functionalities by adding hardware that is designed to plug into Arduino or shields and how to connect several types of displays to Arduino. We'll use several different types of display shields to illustrate the different communication modes that can be used to address the different types of hardware.

A simple serial display

In order to understand how to use a shield, let's start with one of the most basic of the display modules available for Arduino: the serial LCD display. There are several different versions out there, but most provide a simple 2 x 16 character display that can be driven by the serial port on Arduino. This particular display is manufactured by a company called SeeedStudio; other manufacturers make a similar display. It is important that the device documents are compatible with Arduino. This means that the manufacturer has evaluated the unit and is suggesting that it is electrically and mechanically compatible with Arduino. These displays are available at most locations where Arduinos are offered.

The following image shows a picture of the display:

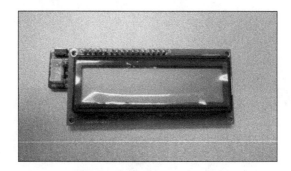

In order to connect this display to your Arduino, perform the following steps:

1. First, you'll need some cabling. In order to connect the LCD to your Arduino, you'll need to add one more cable; this is a four-wire cable that should come with your display, as shown in the following image:

2. Now, you'll need to connect the display to Arduino using these jumper wires. The following image shows a picture of the connection you'll need on the display:

3. The preceding image shows the four pins you need to connect to the display. They are GND and VCC pins, and RX and TX pins from Arduino. The VCC and GND will come from the 5 V and GND pins on Arduino. The RX and TX will come from two pins that you will specify in the code. In this case, looking at the documentation, the code will use pin 11 as RX and pin 12 as TX. So, to connect your Arduino to the display, first plug the four-wire connector into the display; then, use the male-to-male jumpers to connect the four connectors to the proper connections on the board, as shown in the following image:

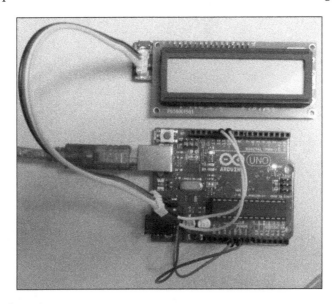

This should complete the hardware connections to the board. You should see the green and red LEDs on the display. This particular type of communication connection is a simple serial connection. The data will be transmitted onto the two pins that you will select in a serial fashion. The display will then take this serial data and translate it to the electrical drive signals needed for the display.

Enabling the serial display in the IDE

Now, let's bring up the Arduino IDE. Before you start coding, you'll need to get the library associated with your display and install it in the IDE.

 For this display, the library is found at http://www.seeedstudio. com/wiki/Grove_-_Serial_LCD. If you go to this website and select the library, it will take you to another web page that will allow you to download a .zip file with the library.

Here are the steps:

1. Download the library. The `.zip` file should then exist in your **Downloads** directory. Now, you'll need to place these files in the **libraries** directory of your Arduino installation. The following screenshot shows the directory structure of the most common installation of the Arduino IDE:

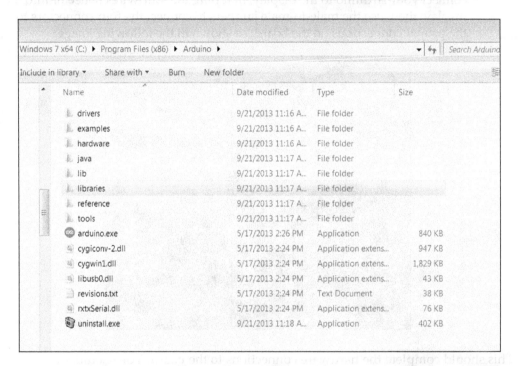

2. Note the location of this directory. Now, go to your **Downloads** directory and unzip the `.zip` file that holds your library. When it asks for the directory to unzip to, select this directory. When complete, this library should be added as a subdirectory in your **libraries** directory, as shown in the following screenshot:

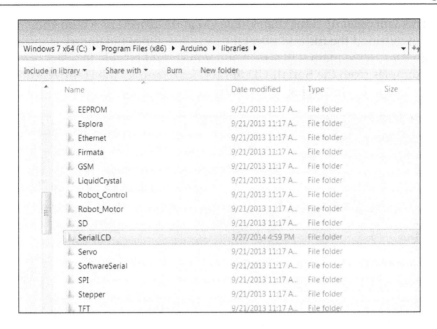

3. Note that the files are in the **libraries** directory under **SerialLCD**. If you'd like to do this automatically, open the Arduino IDE. Select **Sketch**, click on **Import Library...**, and then click on **Add Library...**, as shown in the following screenshot:

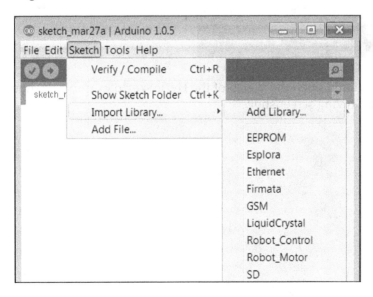

4. This will open up a file dialog box. Go to the directory where you downloaded the file and select the `.zip` file. Once the library is installed, go back to the main IDE screen and you should be able to select one of the examples from the **SerialLCD** library, for example, the **HelloWorld** example, as seen in the following screenshot:

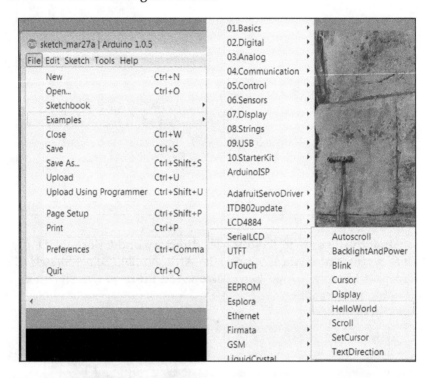

5. This should open the sketch of the **HelloWorld** example. It should look like the following screenshot:

Note that the slcd.print("hello, world!"); statement is the way to send a string text to the serially connected LCD. The slcd.setCursor(0, 1); command sets the cursor to the start of the second line of the display. The slcd.print(millis()/1000); statement is an example of how to print a number to the display, in this case, the number of seconds.

6. Now upload the sketch and you should see the **hello, world!** statement on the display, as shown in the following image:

Now, you can add all sorts of text by simply editing the `slcd.print("hello, world!");` line in the `setup()` function or adding this same function to the `loop()` function. Make sure that if you place a message in the loop, use the `delay(2000)` function after it to give the user some time to read the display before you change it.

Connecting a display using the SPI interface

While the serial display is interesting, it has some limitations. It is difficult to display pictures or graphics, and it is somewhat slower than other interfaces available to you. So, let's add a display with a different communications interface. The following image shows a picture of a small, 1.8 inch LCD module with a micro SD card interface that can be connected to your Arduino:

This particular display is available from a company called SainSmart; it is available directly from the company or other online retailers such as Amazon.com. There are others that are very similar. Finding support for these displays can be difficult, as the interface is significantly more complex; so, check to make sure the libraries are also supplied with the display. To connect to this display, perform the following steps:

1. The first step is to connect the display to your Arduino. The following image shows a picture of the back of the display that will help you connect to the SPI interface on your Arduino:

2. This display uses the SPI interface, so you'll be connecting to the top seven pins shown here. The SI interface is a serial interface but is synchronous, so it provides a more robust communication path. Here is the wiring table that shows which pins to connect to between your Arduino and the display:

Arduino pin	Display pin
+5	VCC
GND	GND
Pin 13	SCL
Pin 11	SDA
Pin 9	RS/DC
Pin 8	RESET
Pin 10	CS

3. To make these connections, you'll want a different type of jumper wire, one with a female connection at one end and a male connection at the other. You can purchase these types of jumper wires at most electronics stores or online.

4. Once the two devices are connected, you can plug your Arduino into the USB cable and the USB cable into your computer; once done, you should see the LCD light up. Now you're ready to add the code.

Enabling the SPI display in the IDE

Just as in the case of SerialLCD, you'll need to add the supporting code library for your device. For this device, the library is found at http://www.sainsmart.com/sainsmart-1-8-spi-lcd-module-with-microsd-led-backlight-for-arduino-mega-atmel-atmega.html. In order to do so, perform the following steps:

1. Go to the site and then click on the **Download** link. This will download the **TFT18.rar** file. Use an archive tool such as **7-Zip** to unpack this file to the **libraries** directory.

2. Now the library will be available for use. You will need to make one change. Go to the library directory where you installed TFT18 and look for a file called ST7735.h, as shown in the following screenshot:

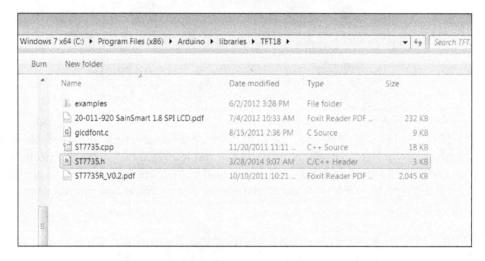

3. You're going to edit the ST7735.h file. You can do that in Notepad if you are working on a Windows system. You are going to change one line, as follows:

```
ST7735.h - Notepad2 (Administrator)
File  Edit  View  Settings  ?
1 // Graphics library by ladyada/adafruit
2 // MIT license
3
4 #define swap(a, b) { uint16_t t = a; a = b; b = t; }
5
6 //#include <WProgram.h>
7 #include <Arduino.h>
8
9 #define ST7735_NOP 0x0
10 #define ST7735_SWRESET 0x01
11 #define ST7735_RDDID 0x04
12 #define ST7735_RDDST 0x09
13
14 #define ST7735_SLPIN   0x10
15 #define ST7735_SLPOUT  0x11
16 #define ST7735_PTLON   0x12
17 #define ST7735_NORON   0x13
18
19 #define ST7735_INVOFF 0x20
20 #define ST7735_INVON 0x21
21 #define ST7735_DISPOFF 0x28
22 #define ST7735_DISPON 0x29
23 #define ST7735_CASET 0x2A
24 #define ST7735_RASET 0x2B
25 #define ST7735_RAMWR 0x2C
26 #define ST7735_RAMRD 0x2E
27
```

4. You are going to comment out the line that reads #include <WProgram.h> using two // characters. Then, you will add the #include <Arduino.h> line as shown in the preceding screenshot. This change is required for the newer Arduino IDE versions.

5. When you have made the change, go back and navigate to **File | Examples | TFT18 | graphicstest**. This will open an example program that will run on your Arduino and drive the display. Upload this, and you should see a graphical set of test patterns on the display, as shown in the following image:

By the way, you may need to exercise a bit of patience; it can take some time for the graphics to display. Now, you can present information on your display. You can also use the example programs under the TFT library as well. Select the **TFTDisplayText** example by navigating to **Examples | TFT | Arduino | TFTDisplayText**. This example program shows you how to display text and a simple number on your display. Here is what this example will look like on the display:

An LCD shield

There is yet another option available to add a display to your projects. The unique part of this solution is that this shield will connect directly to your Arduino, making it a single hardware unit. The concept of a shield is a hardware capability that connects directly into an Arduino board at the header pins available. Connecting this unit is as simple as pressing its connections into the connections on your Arduino. The other nice characteristic of this display is that it comes with a joystick for user input. This unit is available from Amazon.com or other online retailers. The following image shows an LCD shield:

The following image shows a side view of the shield installed into an Arduino board:

Note how the connections on the shield exactly match the proper pins on Arduino. Now that the HW is connected, you can add some code to access the functionality of the shield. Plug your Arduino into the USB cable and the USB cable into the computer. The shield should light up and indicate that power is applied, as shown in the following image:

Enabling the LCD display in the IDE

As with the last two shields, the first step is to add library support for the device. Finding a functional set of libraries for this particular shield is a bit difficult, as this particular shield has been available for some time. Some versions of the libraries for this shield are for older versions of the IDE.

 The correct libraries for Version 1.05 of the Arduino IDE are available at http://www.dfrobot.com/wiki/index.php/ LCD4884_Shield_For_Arduino_%28SKU:DFR0092%29.

To work with this device and the IDE, perform the following steps:

1. Go to the previously mentioned page and navigate to the **Sample Code** section. Right below this is a library selection that, if you select it, will download the library.

2. Now, open the Arduino IDE and select **Sketch**. Click on **Import Library...** and then click on the **LCD4884 V1.2.zip** file. This will import this library into the IDE.

3. Now you can use one of the example programs in your Arduino. To bring up the simplest of these example programs, navigate to **File | Examples | LCD4884 | int_to_String_display**, as shown in the following screenshot:

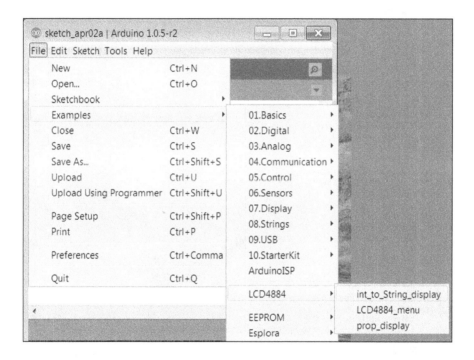

4. This is the simplest set of code to drive the display, and it shows how to display both a string and a number, as shown in the following screenshot:

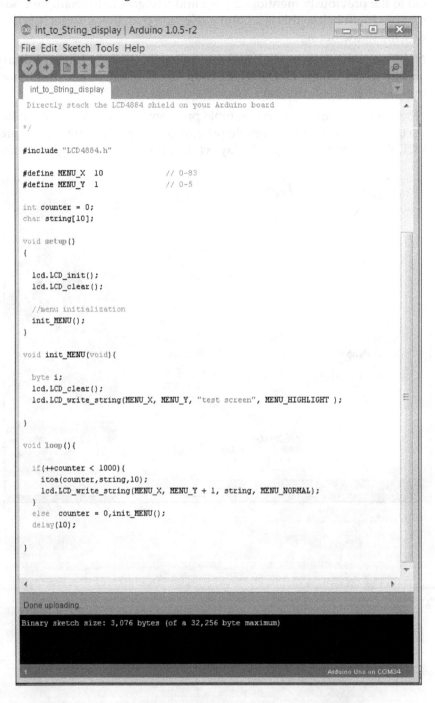

In the preceding example, there are two statements that interface with the graphical display:

- `lcd.LCD-clear();`: This statement initializes and clears the LCD.
- `lcd.LCD_write_string(MENU_X, MENU_Y, "test screen", MENU_HIGHLIGHT)`: This function writes the `test screen` string to the display. The `MENU_X` and `MENU_Y` variables set where the string will be written and the `MENU_HIGHLIGHT` variable causes the string to be in the highlight mode (with a black background and light text).

Here is what the display should look like while running this function:

Now you can use your display to interact with the world. Feel free to check out the other two example programs for more display capabilities and also examples of how to use the joystick.

Summary

That's it! You've learned how to add a display capability to your Arduino projects using serial displays, SPI displays, and a shield with a graphical display. You should experiment with adding all kinds of data, and even using the joystick on the shield. You'll use these same concepts in later chapters to add other types of functionalities. In fact, in the next chapter, you'll use these concepts to control DC motors.

6
Controlling DC Motors

One of the best ways to use Arduino is to add it to a small mobile platform and control the speed and direction of the wheels. In this chapter, you'll learn how to use the basic capability of Arduino to control a small DC motor. You'll then take this to the next level, learning how to add more functionality using a shield to control the speed and direction of more powerful DC motors. Then, we'll build a wheeled robot whose speed and direction are controlled by Arduino.

The basics of DC motor

Before you get started with connecting everything and making it all move, let's spend some time understanding some of the basics of DC motor control. Whether you chose a two or four wheeled mobile platform or a tracked platform, the basic movement control is the same. The unit moves by engaging the motors. If the desired direction is straight, the motors are run at the same speed. If you want to turn the unit, the motors are run at different speeds. The unit can actually turn in a circle if you run one motor forward and one backward.

DC motors are fairly straightforward devices. The speed and direction of the motor is controlled by the magnitude and polarity of the voltage applied to its terminals. The higher the voltage, the faster the motor will turn. If you reverse the polarity of the voltage, you can reverse the direction the motor is turning.

However, the magnitude and polarity of the voltage is not the only factor that is important when you think about controlling your motors. The power that your motor can apply to move your platform is also determined by the voltage and the current supplied at its terminals.

There are actually GPIO pins on Arduino that you could use to create the control voltage and drive your motors directly. The challenge with this method is that Arduino cannot normally source enough current and voltage, and your motors will not be able to generate enough power to move a mobile platform.

There are several solutions to this problem. The first is to use a simple transistor circuit and an external voltage source. You'll use this solution in the first example of this chapter. Another solution is to use an H-bridge, a chip that Arduino can control but which is connected to a power source and can provide enough current. The second example in this chapter will show you how to use this sort of chip. The third solution to the problem is to use a shield that contains all the circuitry and can connect to an external power source input so that your Arduino can provide both voltage and current and your platform can move reliably. The last example in this chapter will use a motor controller shield designed for Arduino to make DC motor control simple.

Connecting a DC motor directly to Arduino

The first step in connecting a DC motor to Arduino is to actually obtain a DC motor. The motors that you will be dealing with here are simple, small DC motors. The motors must not require much current because Arduinos cannot supply more than 40 mA of current directly. For this example, you can use a small 6 V DC motor available at most electronics or hobby stores. The following figure shows one such motor:

In order to connect this motor to your Arduino, you'll need some additional parts. You'll need two male-to-male solderless jumper cables and two alligator clip jumper cables. You'll also need a transistor, a TIP120 to be specific. In this case, the transistor will act like an electronic switch; when you send a control signal to it, the power will flow from the battery. You'll also need a diode, the 1N4004 diode. The diode is a device that protects from reverse power flow. You'll need a 1000 ohm resistor; this will translate the control signal out of Arduino to the proper current for the transistor.

You'll also add a 1 microfarad ceramic capacitor; this capacitor filters out some of the switching noise that can appear on the wires that control the motor. These last four parts should be available at almost any electronics store or online. These parts should be very inexpensive. To control this motor, you'll connect one motor connector to digital pin 11 and the other connector to GND on Arduino. You could use one of the voltage sources on Arduino, but some DC motors can draw lots of current, more than what our Arduino can supply. A safer way is to connect the DC motor supply to a battery holder with four AA batteries.

Connect Arduino, transistor, diode, resistor, and power supply as shown in the following figure:

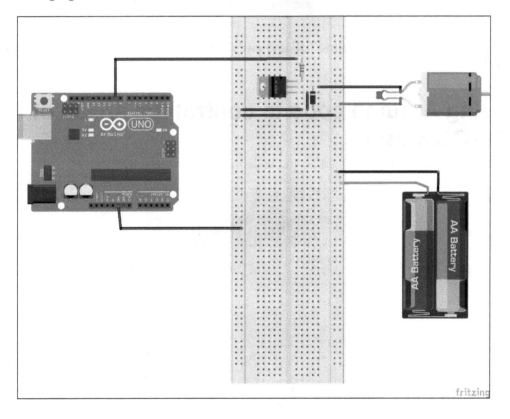

When plugged into the breadboard, the preceding circuit will look like the following figure:

Now, you can start the Arduino IDE and enter a program to send a control signal to the DC motor.

Using Arduino code to control the speed of the DC motor

Now, you'll need to type the following code into the Arduino IDE:

```
int motorPin = 11;
void setup()
{
    pinMode(motorPin, OUTPUT);
    Serial.begin(9600);
    while (! Serial)
        ;
    Serial.println("Set Speed 0 - 255");
}

void loop()
{
    if (Serial.available())
    {
        char str[10];
        int speed = Serial.parseInt();
        itoa(speed, str, 10);
        Serial.println("Speed");
        Serial.println(str);
        if (speed >= 0 && speed <= 255)
        {
            analogWrite(motorPin, speed);
        }
    }
}
```

```
Done uploading.
Binary sketch size: 3,296 bytes (of a 32,256 byte maximum)
```

Now, upload the code to your Arduino. Your motor should start running. Once you have uploaded the code, you'll want to open up the **Serial Monitor** tab so that you can command your motor to run at different speeds. To do this, perform the following steps:

1. First, navigate to **Tools | Serial Monitor**. When you open this, you should see a pop-up window that displays the text from your program as shown in the following screenshot:

2. Enter a value, for example, 255, and then click on **Send**. Your motor should speed up. Now, enter another number, for example, 0, and then click on **Send**. Your motor should stop. Numbers between these two should adjust the speed of your DC motor. Unfortunately, the motor can only go in one direction. The value 255 sends an output to the motor controller that should drive it to its maximum speed, whereas the value 0 sends an output that corresponds with a speed of 0.

The next example will provide a solution if you'd like bidirectional control for your DC motor.

Connecting a DC motor using an H-bridge and Arduino

The next step is to add a bit more functionality with a new type of chip, an H-bridge. An H-bridge is a fairly simple device. It basically consists of a set of switches and adds the additional functionality of allowing the direction of the current to be reversed so that the motor can either be run in the forward or the reverse direction.

Let's start this example by building the H-bridge circuit and controlling just one motor. To do this, you'll need an H-bridge. One of the most common is the L293 dual H-bridge chip. This chip will allow you to control the direction of the DC motors. These are available at most electronics stores or online. You'll also need a capacitor; you can use the 1 microfarad capacitor from the previous example, if you'd like. The capacitor limits the fast changes in the signals that are sent to the motor. Once you have your H-bridge, build the following circuit with Arduino and a breadboard:

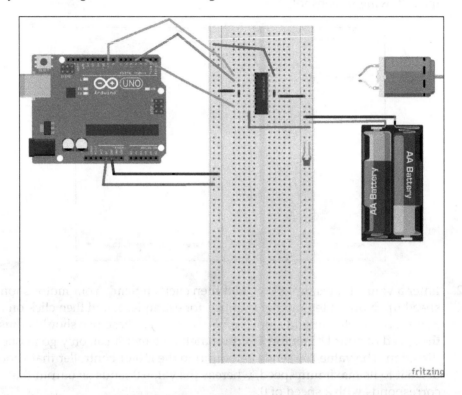

The following table shows Arduino and H-bridge pins and you should connect the pins on Arduino to the pins on the H-bridge:

Arduino pin	H-bridge pin
9	1
4	2
3	7

Once you have the connections, you can test the system. To do that, you'll need to add some code to the code you typed in for example 1.

Using Arduino code to control the direction of the DC motor

Open the Arduino IDE and type in the following code:

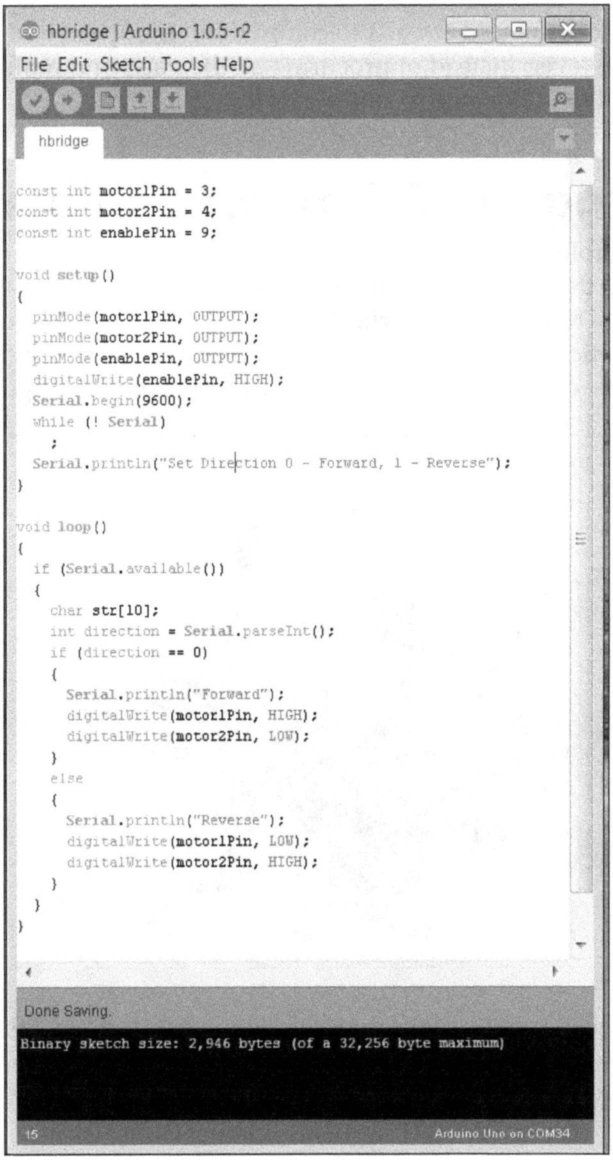

hbridge | Arduino 1.0.5-r2
File Edit Sketch Tools Help
hbridge
const int motor1Pin = 3;
const int motor2Pin = 4;
const int enablePin = 9;
void setup()
{
pinMode(motor1Pin, OUTPUT);
pinMode(motor2Pin, OUTPUT);
pinMode(enablePin, OUTPUT);
digitalWrite(enablePin, HIGH);
Serial.begin(9600);
while (! Serial)
;
Serial.println("Set Direction 0 - Forward, 1 - Reverse");
}
void loop()
{
if (Serial.available())
{
char str[10];
int direction = Serial.parseInt();
if (direction == 0)
{
Serial.println("Forward");
digitalWrite(motor1Pin, HIGH);
digitalWrite(motor2Pin, LOW);
}
else
{
Serial.println("Reverse");
digitalWrite(motor1Pin, LOW);
digitalWrite(motor2Pin, HIGH);
}
}
}
Done Saving.
Binary sketch size: 2,946 bytes (of a 32,256 byte maximum)
15
Arduino Uno on COM34

This code sets up the three pins 3, 4, and 9 to enable the chip and control the direction of the motor. As you did earlier, you can navigate to **Tools | Serial Monitor** to send data to the program. Sending a value of 0 sets pin 3 to HIGH and pin 4 to LOW, causing the motor to spin in one direction. Sending a value of 1 sets pin 3 to LOW and pin 4 to HIGH, causing the motor to spin in the other direction.

Now, you know how to build circuits to control both the speed and the direction of DC motors. However, instead of procuring all the parts and building the circuits yourself, you can buy a DC motor control shield.

Controlling the DC motor using a shield

For this final example, let's graduate from a simple DC motor control circuit to a hardware shield that can control one or two DC motors. For this example, you'll control two DC motors on a wheeled platform. There are several simple, two-wheeled robotic platforms; in this example, you'll use one that is available from several online electronics stores as shown in the following figure:

To make this wheeled robotic platform work, you need to control the two DC motors connected directly to the two wheels. You'll want to control both the direction and the speed of the two wheels to control the direction of the robot.

You'll do this with an Arduino shield designed for this purpose. There are several available; the shield you'll use here is the one available on the Arduino website at www.arduino.cc. The following figure shows the shield:

Specifically, you'll care most about the connections on the front corner of the shield, which is where you will connect the two DC motors. This is shown in the following figure:

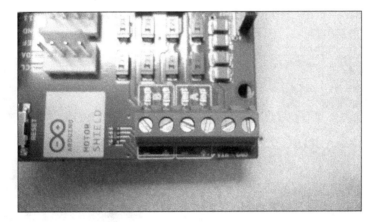

It is these three connections that you will use in this example. First, however, place the board on top of Arduino, in the same way that you placed the display shield from the example in *Chapter 5, Working with Displays*. Then, mount the two boards to the top of your two-wheeled robotic platform, as shown in the following figure:

In this case, I used a large cable tie to mount the boards to the platform and used the foam that came with the motor shield between Arduino and the metal platform. This particular platform comes with a four AA battery holder, so you'll need to connect this power source, or whatever power source you are going to use, to the motor shield. The positive and negative terminals are inserted into the motor shield by loosening the screws, inserting the wires, and then tightening the screws, as shown in the following figure:

Now, you need to connect the motor shield to the motors. If you don't want to solder wires to the motors, you can use the alligator clip wires as shown in the following figure:

The final step is to connect the alligator clip wires to the motor controller shield. I did this with the male-to-male solderless jumper wires. First, insert the cables into the motor shield screw connectors. There are two sets of connections—one for each motor. Then, attach the alligator clips to the other ends of these wires as shown in the following figure:

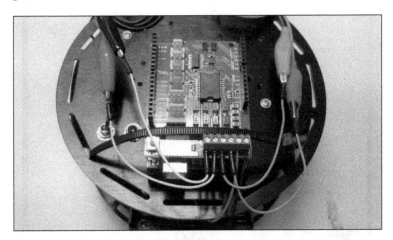

Insert some batteries, and then connect Arduino to the computer via the USB cable. Now, you are ready to start programming to control the motors.

The Arduino code for the DC motor shield

Now that the HW is in place, bring up the Arduino IDE; make sure that the proper port and device are selected and enter the following code:

```
wheeledplatform | Arduino 1.0.5-r2

File Edit Sketch Tools Help

wheeledplatform §

int pwmA = 3;
int pwmB = 11;
int brakeA = 9;
int brakeB = 8;
int directionA = 12;
int directionB = 13;

void setup() {
  pinMode(directionA, OUTPUT);
  pinMode(brakeA, OUTPUT);
  pinMode(directionB, OUTPUT);
  pinMode(brakeB, OUTPUT);
}

void loop(){
// Move Forward
  digitalWrite(directionA, HIGH);
  digitalWrite(brakeA, LOW);
  analogWrite(pwmA, 255);
  digitalWrite(directionB, HIGH);
  digitalWrite(brakeB, LOW);
  analogWrite(pwmB, 255);
  delay(2000);

  digitalWrite(brakeA, HIGH);
  digitalWrite(brakeB, HIGH);
  delay(1000);

  //Turn Right
  digitalWrite(directionA, LOW); //Establishes backward direction of Channel A
  digitalWrite(brakeA, LOW); //Disengage the Brake for Channel A
  analogWrite(pwmA, 128); //Spins the motor on Channel A at half speed
  digitalWrite(directionB, HIGH); //Establishes forward direction of Channel B
  digitalWrite(brakeB, LOW); //Disengage the Brake for Channel B
  analogWrite(pwmB, 128); //Spins the motor on Channel B at full speed
  delay(2000);
  digitalWrite(brakeA, HIGH);
  digitalWrite(brakeB, HIGH);
  delay(1000);
}
```

23   Arduino Uno on COM18

The code is straightforward. It consists of the following three blocks:

- The declaration of the six variables that connect to the proper Arduino pins are as follows:

```
int pwmA = 3;
int pwmB = 11;
int brakeA = 9;
int brakeB = 8;
int directionA = 12;
int directionB = 13;
```

- The `setup()` function, which sets the `directionA`, `directionB`, `brakeA`, and `brakeB` digital output pins:

```
pinMode(directionA, OUTPUT);
pinMode(brakeA, OUTPUT);
pinMode(directionB, OUTPUT);
pinMode(brakeB, OUTPUT);
```

- The `loop()` function. This is an example of how to make the wheeled robot go forward and then turn to the right. At each of these steps, you'll need to use the brake to stop the robot. The code is as follows:

```
// Move forward
digitalWrite(directionA, HIGH);
digitalWrite(brakeA, LOW);
analogWrite(pwmA, 255);
digitalWrite(directionB, HIGH);
digitalWrite(brakeB, LOW);
analogWrite(pwmB, 255);

delay(2000);

digitalWrite(brakeA, HIGH);
digitalWrite(brakeB, HIGH);

delay(1000);

//Turn right
digitalWrite(directionA, LOW); //Establishes backward direction of
Channel A
digitalWrite(brakeA, LOW); //Disengage the Brake for Channel A
analogWrite(pwmA, 128); //Spins the motor on Channel A at half
speed
```

```
digitalWrite(directionB, HIGH); //Establishes forward direction of
Channel B
digitalWrite(brakeB, LOW); //Disengage the Brake for Channel B
analogWrite(pwmB, 128); //Spins the motor on Channel B at full
speed
delay(2000);
digitalWrite(brakeA, HIGH);
digitalWrite(brakeB, HIGH);

delay(1000);
```

Once you have uploaded the code, the program should run in a loop. If you want to run your robot without connection to the computer, place batteries into the battery holder, disconnect the USB cable connecting Arduino to the computer, and then press the **RESET** button. Your robot can move all by itself!

Summary

By now, you should be feeling a bit more comfortable with configuring HW and writing code for Arduino. Hopefully, your wheeled platform is moving around and is controlled by Arduino. You've learned the basics of DC motor control, and in the process, you also learned how to send control signals to the external hardware.

In the next chapter, you'll change this platform from one based on DC motors to one based on servos, and you'll build a robot that can walk.

7
Controlling Servos with Arduino

In this chapter, you'll learn how to use the basic capability of Arduino to control servo motors.

Servo motors are important because you can use them to create all kinds of useful arms, legs, or even pan-and-tilt mechanisms to make really cool robots that can walk, or pick up things, or move sensors around. You'll then take this to the next level, learning how to add more functionality using a shield to control the speed and direction of a whole set of servos to build a walking hexapod robot.

The basics of a servo motor

Before you begin, you'll need some background on servo motors. Servo motors are somewhat similar to DC motors; however, there is an important difference. While DC motors are generally designed to move in a continuous way—rotating 360 degrees at a given speed—servos are generally designed to move within a limited set of angles. In other words, in the DC motor world, you generally want your motors to spin with continuous rotation speed that you control. In the servo motor world, you want your motor to move to a specific position that you control.

Controlling servos is fairly simple. The device has three wires connected to it: one for the ground connection, one for the drive voltage, and the third is a control signal that expects a **pulse-width modulated (PWM)** signal. The signal is a square wave that is turned on and off at a set rate, normally at around 500 Hz. The ratio of the length of the time the signal is on to the time the signal is off determines the desired angle of the servo.

Arduino can control servos using two different approaches. The first is to connect your servos directly to Arduino. You'll use this solution in the first example of this chapter. Unfortunately, if you have a lot of servo motors, they can sometimes draw more current than Arduino can provide, which is 40 mA. To solve this problem, you'll need to use a shield that can connect to an external power source. Then, your Arduino and shield can provide both voltage and current so that you can control many servos. The second example in this chapter will use this servo controller shield designed for Arduino to control 12 servos on a hexapod robot.

Connecting a servo motor directly to Arduino

The first step in connecting a servo motor to Arduino is to actually obtain a servo motor. The following figure shows a typical servo motor, the Hitec HS-311, available at most hobby or RC Control stores:

In order to connect this servo motor to your Arduino, you'll need some of those male-to-male solderless jumper cables that you used in the previous chapters. You'll notice that there are three wires coming from the servo. Two of these supply the voltage and current to the servo. The third provides a control signal that tells the servo where and how to move. You'll connect these three wires to the pins on Arduino. The black wire on the servo is ground; you'll connect that to the GND pin on Arduino. The red wire on the servo is the VCC connection; connect that to the 5 V pin on Arduino. The orange pin is the control pin on the servo; connect that to one of the DIGITAL (PWM~) pins on Arduino, for example, pin 11, as shown in the following figure:

Just a word of caution, this works well with a single servo; you will not want to use the method for more than just one or two servos. Now that you have made these connections, you are ready to write the code to make your servo move.

Controlling the servos with a program

Now that the hardware is connected, you'll need to supply the control signal to make your servos move. To control your servo, bring up the Arduino IDE. Make sure that the proper Arduino and port are chosen. Then enter the lines of code as shown in the following screenshot:

This code uses the `Servo` library that is installed with the standard Arduino IDE. The three sections of code that you'll need to understand are as follows:

- The global variables `servo`, `servoPin`, and `angle` are used by the program. The `Servo` data type adds a set of functions so that you can control your servo. This includes the `servo.attach(servoPin)` and `servo.write(angle)` functions, which you will use in this program to send the servo to a specific angle. To find out all the different functions that are available, visit `http://arduino.cc/en/reference/servo`.

- The `setup()` function connects the servo functionality to the proper pin and then initializes the serial port.

- The `loop()` function reads the serial port, and then uses that data to send the servo to the proper angle by using `servo.write(angle)`.

When you have entered the code, upload the program. When it runs, navigate to **Tools | Serial Monitor**. You can then enter the desired angle, as shown in the following screenshot:

Now you can imagine adding a whole set of servos, one controlled by a different digital output pin on Arduino. However, Arduino itself will soon run out of the ability to supply enough current to control more servos. So if you have projects that require more than just one or two servos, you'll probably want to go with a servo motor shield.

Connecting a servo motor shield to Arduino

The servo motor shield we'll use in this example is available at most online retailers who sell Arduino Uno, and is made by AdaFruit. The following figure shows the servo motor shield connected to the servo wires:

This particular shield can handle up to 16 servos. The important characteristic of this servo shield is the connection on the right-hand side of the shield. In the GND and VCC connections, you'll place your external voltage and current input, allowing Arduino to control many more servos.

Controlling the servo motor shield with a program

Now that your hardware is ready, you'll need to program Arduino to send the proper control signals. To control this shield, you'll need to download a library from Adafruit.

 The library for the motor shield can be downloaded from https://learn.adafruit.com/adafruit-16-channel-pwm-slash-servo-shield/using-the-adafruit-library.

Once you have downloaded the library, you'll need to rename it to install it into the IDE. Look for the `Adafruit-PWM-Servo-Driver-Library-master.zip` file in the directory you downloaded the file from, and unzip this to the directory where your Arduino library is stored, as shown in the following screenshot:

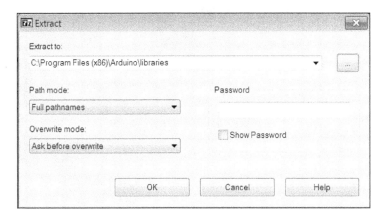

The `Adafruit-PWM-Servo-Driver-Library-master` directory should now be in the `library` directory. You'll need to change the name of this directory to `AdafruitServoDriver`. The library and its examples are now available. You can open the servo example by navigating to **File** | **Examples** | **AdafruitServoDriver** | **servo**, as shown in the following screenshot:

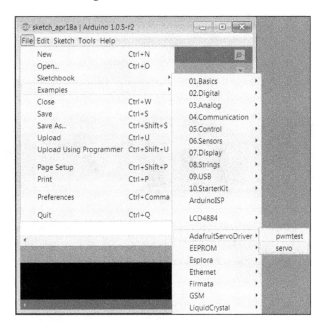

Then, you should be able to see the code snippet as shown in the following screenshot:

This code is well documented, and shows you how to drive each individual servo. However, this isn't the most exciting application. What you really want is to build a legged quadruped robot to exercise all of these servos.

To complete this project, you'll first need to buy some parts so you can build your quadruped robot. There are several possibilities out there, but one set I personally like is a set of Lynxmotion parts available from the online retailer `robotshop.com`. To build your quadruped robot, you'll need two sets each of the two leg parts, and then one set each of a body part. The following table illustrates the parts as they are listed on the website:

Quantity	Description
1	Lynxmotion Symmetric Quadrapod Body Kit-Mini QBK-02
2	Lynxmotion 3" Aluminum Femur Pair
2	Lynxmotion Robot Leg "A" Pair (No Servo) RL-01
4	Lynxmotion Aluminum Multi-Purpose Servo Bracket Two Pack ASB-04

Once you have these parts, you'll also need 12 standard size servos. I personally like the Hitec servos; they are a very inexpensive servo that you can get at most hobby shops and online electronics retailers. You may need quite a powerful servo, so buy at least the HS-422. When you get the parts, perform the following steps:

1. Put two right legs together, as shown in the following figure:

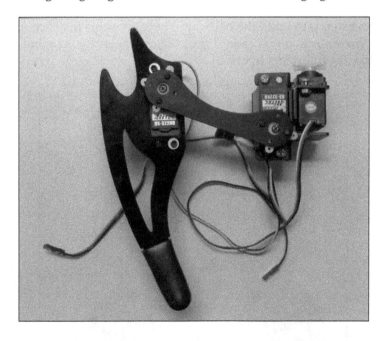

2. Now, put two left legs together as shown in the following figure:

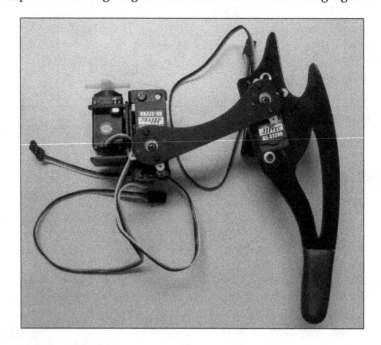

3. The next step is to build the body kit. There are some instructions at
   `www.lynxmotion.com/images/html/sq3u-assembly.htm`, but it should
   look like the following figure:

4. And then connect each leg to the body kit. The important part of this step is to make sure you use a bearing on the underside connection of the leg, as shown in the following figure:

5. The final step is to mount the batteries and Arduino to the body kit, as shown in the following figure:

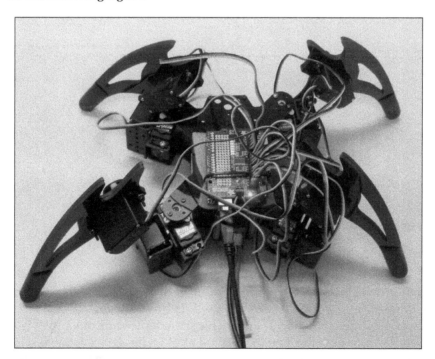

I like to use an RC LiPo battery for my robotic projects; they are available from most RC stores or online. You can certainly use standard alkaline AA batteries, but they are not rechargeable and don't last very long. Using rechargeable AA batteries solves the rechargeable problem, so it is certainly a better choice. I find the RC LiPo batteries last the longest and recharge quickest. If you are going to use a LiPo battery, choose a 2S battery; this will provide 7.4 V, which will then be regulated by the Arduino and can drive both Arduino and servos. Your kit is now ready to move. Let's start with a simple program that sets all of the servos to their middle position, and then takes in a command to move just one of the servos to a specific angle. This will help you understand how your robot is configured, as shown in the following screenshot:

The preceding code includes a significant number of `Serial.println()` functions; these are there to show you what is happening. The key statement for servo control is `pwm.setPWM(servo, 0, pwmValue);`. This statement sends out a PWM signal that the servo motor uses to determine the desired angle. The `servo` variable selects the servo to control, the `0` variable sets when the PWM pulse starts (you'll use 0 for this application), and the `pwmValue` variable sets the length of the pulse. You can now see how your robot can be programmed to be moved by performing the following steps:

1. One step you'll probably want to do is adjust the mechanical position of your servos. To do this, run the program so that all of the servos are set to their middle location.

2. Then, unscrew the screw at the center of each horn connected to the servo, and turn it so that it is now in the middle location on the robot for that particular servo.

When your robot is centered, you can now begin to program your robot to do things. First, let's add a command that waves one of the front legs. From the Arduino sketch, change your `loop()` function, and add the `home()` and `wave()` functions, as shown in the code snippet in the following screenshot:

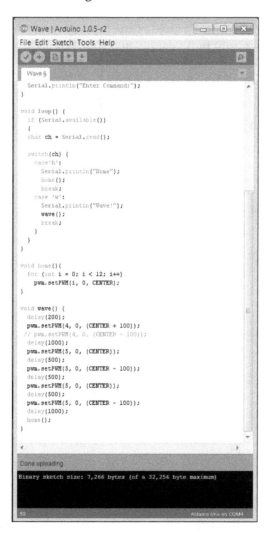

The code is very simple; the `setup()` function establishes your access to the servo shield and the loop simply takes in a command from the serial port, and when it sees from the Serial Monitor tab, it moves the front leg up and down three times.

You can really take advantage of the SW that is available out there, as there is a set of SW capabilities that have been created by enterprising individuals that will allow your quadruped robot to do a number of different actions based on the input from the serial port. One example is at `letsmakerobots.com/node/35354` and another at `blog.oscarliang.net/arduino-quadruped-robot-stalker/`.

Summary

You have learned how to control a single servo and an entire set with a servo control shield. Now you can not only build robots that role, but you can also build robots that walk. You know how to easily add even more servos to act as arms, or any number of other functions. However, your robot really can't sense the outside world yet, and is reliant entirely upon someone to control it.

In the next chapter, you'll add sensors so that your robot can avoid/find obstacles and other objects.

8
Avoiding Obstacles Using Sensors

Now that your robot can move, it is important to make sure it won't run into walls or other barriers. In this chapter, you'll learn the following topics:

- How to add sensors to your projects
- How to add a servo to your sensor

An overview of the sensors

Before you begin, you'll need to decide which sensors to use. You require basic sensors that will return information about the distance to an object, and there are two choices—sonar and infrared. Let's look at each.

Sonar sensors

The sonar sensor uses ultrasonic sound to calculate the distance to an object. The sensor consists of a transmitter and receiver. The transmitter creates a sound wave that travels out from the sensor, as illustrated in the following diagram:

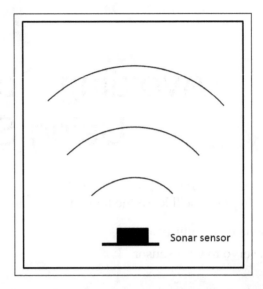

The device sends out a sound wave 10 times a second. If an object is in the path of these waves, the waves reflect off the object. This then returns sound waves to the sensor, as shown in the following diagram:

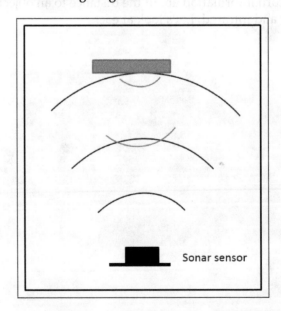

The sensor measures the returning sound waves. It uses the time difference between when the sound wave was sent out and when it returns to measure the distance to the object.

Infrared sensors

Another type of sensor is a sensor that uses **infrared** (**IR**) signals to detect distance. An IR sensor also uses both a transmitter and a receiver. The transmitter transmits a narrow beam of light and the sensor receives this beam of light. The difference in transit ends up as an angle measurement at the sensor, as shown in the following diagram:

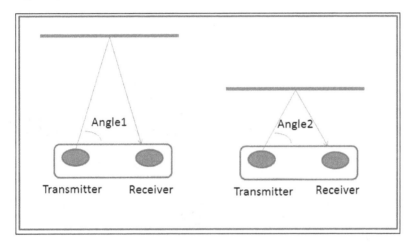

The different angles give you an indication of the distance to the object. Unfortunately, the relationship between the output of the sensor and the distance is not linear, so you'll need to do some calibration to predict the actual distance and its relationship to the output of the sensor. This will be discussed later in this chapter.

Connecting a sonar sensor to Arduino

Here is an image of a sonar sensor, HC-SR04, which works well with Arduino:

These sonar sensors are available at most places that sell Arduino products, including amazon.com. In order to connect this sonar sensor to your Arduino, you'll need some of those female-to-male jumper cables that you used in the previous chapters. You'll notice that there are four pins to connect the sonar sensor. Two of these supply the voltage and current to the sensor. One pin, the Trig pin, triggers the sensor to send out a sound wave. The Echo pin then senses the return from the echo.

To access the sensor with Arduino, make the following connections using the male-to-female jumper wires:

Arduino pin	Sensor pin
5V	Vcc
GND	GND
12	Trig
11	Echo

Accessing the sonar sensor from the Arduino IDE

Now that the HW is connected, you'll want to download a library that supports this sensor. One of the better libraries for this sensor is available at https://code.google.com/p/arduino-new-ping/. Download the NewPing library and then open the Arduino IDE. You can include the library in the IDE by navigating to **Sketch** | **Import Library** | **Add Library** | **Downloads** and selecting the NewPing ZIP file. Once you have the library installed, you can access the example program by navigating to **File** | **Examples** | **NewPing** | **NewPingExample** as shown in the following screenshot:

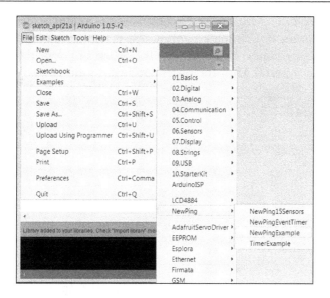

You will then see the following code in the IDE:

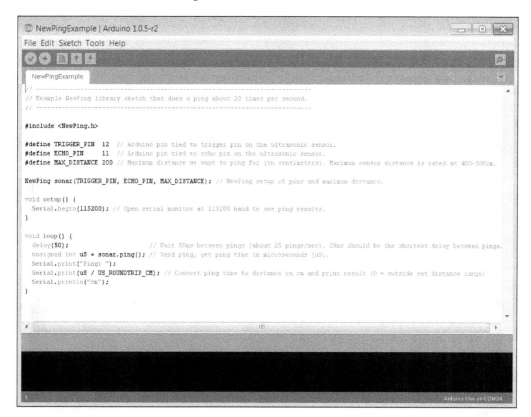

Now, upload the code to Arduino and open a serial terminal by navigating to **Tools | Serial Monitor** in the IDE. Initially, you will see characters that make no sense; you need to change the serial port baud rate to **115200 baud** by selecting this field in the lower-right corner of **Serial Monitor**, as shown in the following screenshot:

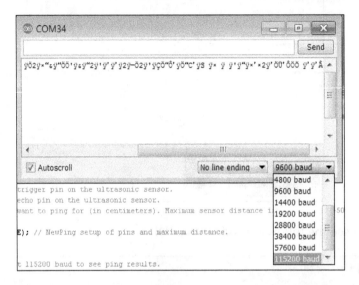

Now, you should begin to see results that make sense. If you place your hand in front of the sensor and then move it, you should see the distance results change, as shown in the following screenshot:

You can now measure the distance to an object using your sonar sensor.

Connecting an IR sensor to Arduino

One popular choice is the Sharp series of IR sensors. Here is an image of one of the models, Sharp 2Y0A02, which is a unit that provides sensing to a distance of 150 cm:

To connect this unit, you'll need to connect the three pins that are available on the bottom of the sensor. Here is the connection list:

Arduino pin	Sensor pin
5V	Vcc
GND	GND
A3	Vo

Unfortunately, there are no labels on the unit, but there is a data sheet that you can download from www.phidgets.com/documentation/Phidgets/3522_0_Datasheet.pdf. The following image shows the pins you'll need to connect:

One of the challenges of making this connection is that the female-to-male connection jumpers are too big to connect directly to the sensor. You'll want to order the three-wire cable with connectors with the sensor, and then you can make the connections between this cable and your Arduino device using the male-to-male jumper wires. Once the pins are connected, you are ready to access the sensor via the Arduino IDE.

Accessing the IR sensor from the Arduino IDE

Now, bring up the Arduino IDE. Here is a simple sketch that provides access to the sensor and returns the distance to the object via the serial link:

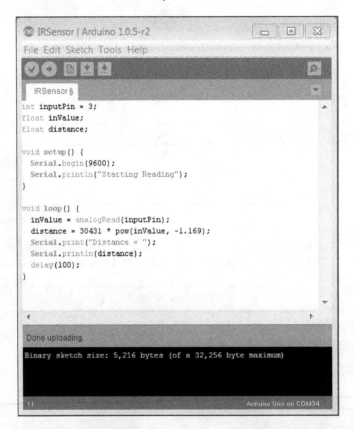

The sketch is quite simple. The three global variables at the top set the input pin to A3 and provide a storage location for the input value and distance. The `setup()` function simply sets the serial port baud rate to `9600` and prints out a single line to the serial port.

In the `loop()` function, you first get the value from the A3 input port. The next step is to convert it to a distance based on the voltage. To do this, you need to use the voltage to distance chart for the device; in this case, it is similar to the following diagram:

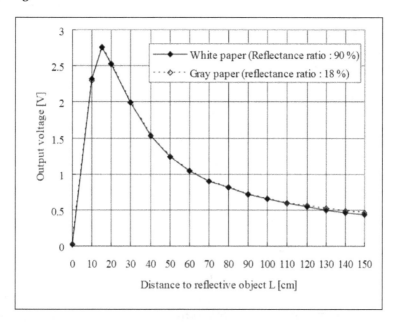

There are two parts to the curve. The first is the distance up to about 15 centimeters and then the distance from 15 centimeters to 150 centimeters. This simple example ignores distances closer than 15 centimeters, and models the distance from 15 centimeters and out as a decaying exponential with the following form:

$$constant * input\ value - exponential\ value$$

Thanks to `teaching.ericforman.com/how-to-make-a-sharp-ir-sensor-linear/`, the values that work quite well for a cm conversion in distance are 30431 for the constant and -1.169 as the exponential for this curve.

If you open the **Serial Monitor** tab and place an object in front of the sensor, you'll see the readings for the distance to the object, as shown in the following screenshot:

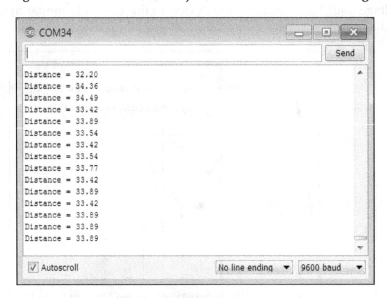

By the way, when you place the object closer than 15 cm, you should begin to see distances that seem much larger than should be indicated. This is due to the voltage to distance curve at these much shorter distances. If you truly need very short distances, you'll need a much more complex calculation.

Creating a scanning sensor platform

While knowing the distance in front of your robotic project is normally important, you might want to know other distances around the robot as well. One solution is to hook up multiple sensors, which is quite simple. However, there is another solution that may be a bit more cost effective. Instead of multiple sensors, you can place a single sensor on a servo and then use the concepts that you learned in *Chapter 7, Controlling Servos with Arduino*, to move the servo and allow the sensor to scan a set of different distances.

To create a scanning sensor of this type, take a sensor of your choice (in this case, I'll use the IR sensor) and mount it on a servo. I like to use a servo L bracket for this, which is mounted on the servo Pas follows:

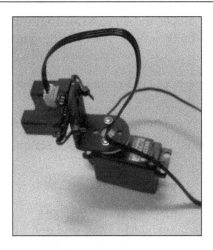

You'll need to connect both the IR sensor (as described earlier in this chapter) as well as the servo to Arduino (as explained in *Chapter 7, Controlling Servos with Arduino*).

Now, you will need some Arduino code that will move the servo and also take the sensor readings. The following screenshot illustrates the code:

```
basicServoIR | Arduino 1.0.5-r2
File Edit Sketch Tools Help

basicServoIR

#include <Servo.h>
Servo servo;
int servoPin = 11;
int angle = 0;
int inputPin = 3;
float inValue;
float distance;

void setup()
{
  servo.attach(servoPin);
  Serial.begin(9600);
  Serial.println("Set Angle 0 to 180");
}

void loop()
{
  if (Serial.available())
  {
    char str[10];
    angle = Serial.parseInt();
    itoa(angle, str, 10);
    Serial.println("Angle ");
    Serial.println(str);
    if (angle >= 0 && angle <= 180)
    {
      servo.write(angle);
      delay(1000);
      inValue = analogRead(inputPin);
      distance = 30431 * pow(inValue, -1.169);
      Serial.print("Distance = ");
      Serial.println(distance);
    }
  }
}
```

Done Saving

Arduino Uno en COM14

The preceding code simply moves the servo to an angle and then prints out the distance value reported by the IR sensor. The specific statements that may be of interest are as follows:

- `servo.attach(servoPin);`: This statement attaches the servo control to the pin defined

- `servo.write(angle);`: This statement sends the servo to this angle

- `inValue = analogRead(inputPin);`: This statement reads the analog input value from this pin

- `distance = 30431 * pow(inValue, -1.169);`: This statement translates the reading to distance in centimeters

If you upload the sketch, open **Serial Monitor**, and enter different angle values, the servo should move and you should see something like the following screenshot:

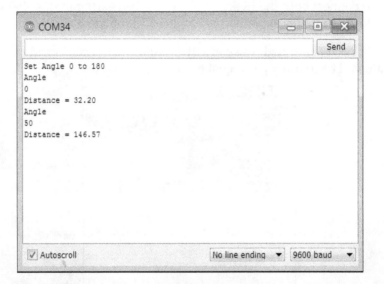

Summary

Now that you know how to use sensors to understand the environment, you can create even more complex programs that will sense these barriers and then change the direction of your robot to avoid them or collide with them. You learned how to find distance using sonar sensors and how to connect them to Arduino. You also learned about IR sensors and how they can be used with Arduino.

In the next chapter, you'll learn how to add even more interesting sensors, such as a digital compass, so that you can plan your travel routes even more efficiently.

9
Even More Useful Sensors

Your projects may want to do more than just avoiding barriers. In this chapter, we'll go through the following topics:

- How to add a digital compass so that your projects can sense direction.
- How to add an accelerometer/gyro to your project so that you can sense the tilt and movement of your projects.
- How to add an altimeter/pressure sensor to your project so that you can sense your altitude. These can also be useful in weather prediction.

Connecting a digital compass to Arduino

One of the important pieces of information that might be useful for your robot is its direction of travel. This could be given by a GPS unit, and we will cover how to connect one of those in *Chapter 11, Using a GPS Device with Arduino*. However, a GPS unit can be expensive, and it often doesn't work well inside buildings, because the GPS satellite signals don't penetrate buildings well. So, let's learn how to hook up a digital compass to Arduino.

There are several chips that provide digital compass capability; one of the most common ones is the **HMC5883L 3-Axis Digital Compass chip**. This chip is packaged onto a module by several companies, but almost all of them result in a similar interface. Here is a picture of one by a company called SainSmart, and it is available at a number of online retailers:

This type of digital compass uses magnetic sensors to discover the earth's magnetic field. The output of these sensors is then made accessible to the outside world through a set of registers that allow the user to set things such as the sample rate and continuous or single sampling. The x, y, and z directions are output using registers as well.

The connections to this chip are straightforward; the device communicates with Arduino using the I2C bus, a standard serial communications bus.

The I2C interface is a synchronous serial interface and provides more performance than an asynchronous Rx/Tx serial interface. The SCL data line provides a clock, while the data flows on the SDA line. The bus also provides addressing so that more than one device can be connected to the master device at the same time.

On the back of the module, the connections are labeled as follows:

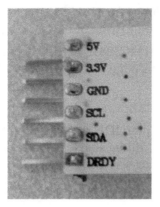

The following are the connections that you'll need to make between Arduino and the device:

Arduino pin	Sensor pin
5V	5V
GND	GND
A5	SCL
A4	SDA

Notice that you will not connect the 3.3V or DRDY (data ready) lines. Our Arduino supplies power through the 5V line instead of the 3.3V line, and the DRDY line is not needed by this library. Now, you are ready to talk with the device using the IDE.

Accessing the compass from the Arduino IDE

The first step in accessing the compass capability from the IDE is to install a library. Finding a library that supports the module is a bit difficult, but one that works well is available at www.emartee.com/product/42254/HMC5883L%203%20Axis%20 Digital%20Compass%20Module.

The following are the steps to install the library and run the example:

1. Select the **Arduino Library for HMC5883L** link on the previously mentioned page, and it will take you to a set of library selections.

2. You need to select the **HMC5883L / HMC5883L Library For Arduino.rar** link at the bottom of this page, and it will download a .rar file that holds the library.

3. Unzip this file into the libraries directory of your Arduino installation.

4. Now, bring up the Arduino IDE and select the **Examples** option under the **File** menu, and you should be able to select the HMC5883L library example, as shown in the following screenshot:

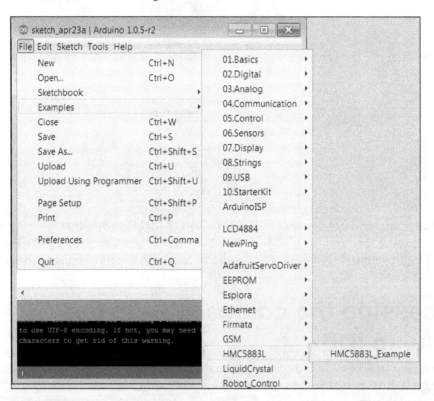

5. Once you have selected this example, upload it to your Arduino and open the Serial Monitor. You may have to resize the monitor to get a good look at the results, but you should see something similar to the following screenshot:

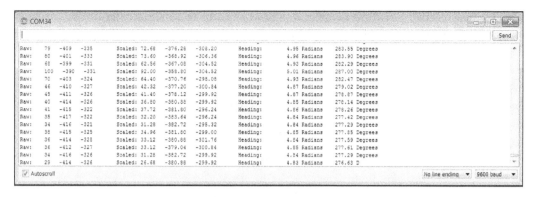

The `Raw` data is the x, y, and z data that is coming directly from the compass and is related directly to the earth's magnetic field. The `Scaled` values are those that are scaled to reflect true north. The `Heading` value is expressed in degrees and radians. Now, you can add direction to your project! As you move the device around, you should see the `Heading` value change. These readings should give you an indication of the heading of your project. This is very useful to help you give direction to your robotic projects. However, you may want to use even more information, such as speed and tilt. Fortunately, there are sensors for this as well.

Connecting an accelerometer/gyro to Arduino

The ability to measure speed and tilt is important in many robotic applications. You'll need to add an accelerometer/gyro sensor for this. This device measures the tilt using very small gyros, devices that spin and resist changes in orientation. When these changes occur, the resistance to change can be measured. The device also measures movement using an accelerometer. An accelerometer measures movement in one direction using very small (MEMS) machines that respond to motion by outputting a small signal.

Providing this information can help you know how your device is moving. Fortunately, there are chips that can provide this functionality. One of them is the **MPU-6050** chip, which provides a complete set of information on movement, including the acceleration and tilt. There are several different manufacturers who place this chip on a small board accessible from Arduino.

One of these is the SparkFun version, the SparkFun SEN-11028, available at `sparkfun.com`. It is shown in the following image:

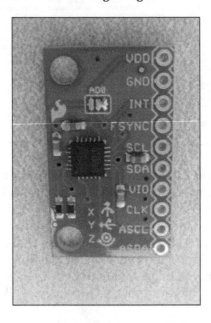

The interface to the board is quite simple, with only one issue. One of the ways to connect this particular chip is to solder header pins to the board to connect the jumper wires to Arduino. You can purchase these at `sparkfun.com` as well; just search for the Arduino stackable header, 8-pin version. Once the header is soldered, the device will look as follows:

Now, you can use a male-to-male jumper cable to connect between Arduino and the board. The following table shows the connections:

Arduino pin	Sensor pin
3.3V	VDD
GND	GND
A5	SCL
A4	SDA
3.3V	VIO

You'll notice that you need to make two connections to the 3.3V supply, so you may want to create a male-to-male jumper cable with two connections on one end. This can be done using three male-to-male cables. For this, we need to cut off one end and strip back the insulation, then solder the three cables together, and then wrap the solder connection in electrical tape.

Accessing the accelerometer from the Arduino IDE

Now that the two devices are connected, you'll need to bring up the Arduino IDE and add a library so that you can access the functionality from the SW. Follow these steps:

1. Go to github.com/jrowberg/i2cdevlib and look on the right-hand side of the page for the download link. This will download the entire library.

 From the SparkFun page on the device at www.sparkfun.com/products/11028, you'll find a GitHub repository that supports not only this device, but a number of devices that use the I2C interface.

2. Now, you should unzip the file to a handy location; I unzipped mine in the `Downloads` directory. What you want is just the files associated with Arduino, so go to the directory that supports those files, as shown in the following screenshot:

Downloads ▸ i2cdevlib-master ▸ i2cdevlib-master ▸ Arduino ▸		
Share with ▾ Burn New folder		
Name	Date modified	Type
_Stub	4/23/2014 4:56 PM	File folder
AD7746	4/23/2014 4:56 PM	File folder
ADS1115	4/23/2014 4:56 PM	File folder
ADXL345	4/23/2014 4:56 PM	File folder
AK8975	4/23/2014 4:56 PM	File folder
BMA150	4/23/2014 4:56 PM	File folder
BMP085	4/23/2014 4:56 PM	File folder
DS1307	4/23/2014 4:56 PM	File folder
HMC5843	4/23/2014 4:56 PM	File folder
HMC5883L	4/23/2014 4:56 PM	File folder
I2Cdev	4/23/2014 4:56 PM	File folder
IAQ2000	4/23/2014 4:56 PM	File folder
ITG3200	4/23/2014 4:56 PM	File folder
L3G4200D	4/23/2014 4:56 PM	File folder
LM73	4/23/2014 4:56 PM	File folder
MPR121	4/23/2014 4:56 PM	File folder
MPU6050	4/23/2014 4:56 PM	File folder
SSD1308	4/23/2014 4:56 PM	File folder
TCA6424A	4/23/2014 4:56 PM	File folder

3. Even though you won't need all of these libraries right now, you can just copy all of these to your `Libraries` directory of your Arduino for future use. You'll notice, by the way, that there is a duplicate of the `HMC5883L` library you installed earlier, so you can decide to merge these directories.

4. Once you have these directories installed, bring up the Arduino IDE. Before you bring up the example program for the device, open the Serial Monitor and set the baud rate to `38400`. Now, bring up the example program that reads the raw values of the accelerometer and gyro by navigating to **Examples** | **MPU6050** | **Examples** | **MPU6050_raw**, as shown in the following screenshot:

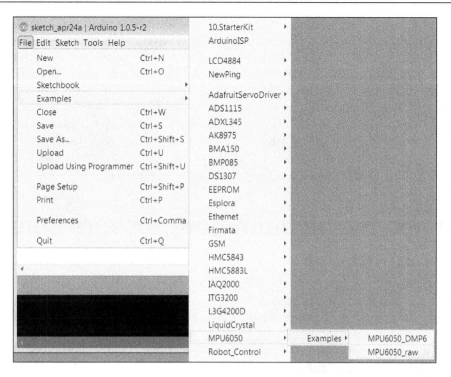

This will open a sketch that provides the code to read the raw data from your sensor. When you upload the code and open the Serial Monitor, you should see something similar to the following screenshot:

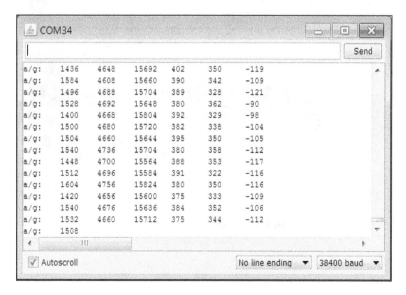

The first three numbers are the x, y, and z raw accelerometer readings, and the last three are the x, y, and z angle readings from the gyroscope. If you mount the device flat in your project, the x, y, and z readings would be associated with the yaw, pitch, and roll of the device respectively. As you move the device around, you should see these readings change. This data can then be used to sense when your device is moving, in what direction, and how it is positioned. The device has a lot of capabilities, including the ability to calibrate itself so that a particular position is the "zero" position. For more information about these capabilities, feel free to look at both example programs provided by the library. In *Chapter 13*, *Robots That Can Fly*, you'll learn how to use this device in a quad-copter application.

Connecting an altimeter/pressure sensor to Arduino

The final sensor that you'll learn about in this chapter is the altimeter/pressure sensor. An altimeter measures the barometric pressure, and as this pressure decreases with rising elevation, it can indicate elevation. This is particularly useful when you want to build a robot that can fly. First, you'll need to select a device. One device that can provide this information is the SainSmart BMP085 Module Digital Barometric Pressure Sensor, available at many online retailers. It looks as follows:

It looks very similar to the digital compass, and just like the earlier two devices, it connects via the I2C interface. You can even use the same libraries you just downloaded for the accelerometer/gyro for I2C support.

The connections between Arduino and the device will be the same as the digital compass, as demonstrated in the following table:

Arduino pin	Sensor pin
5V	5V
GND	GND
A5	SCL
A4	SDA

The connections, just like those of the digital compass, are clearly marked on the back of the device, and you can use female-to-male jumpers to make the connections.

Accessing the altimeter/pressure sensor from the Arduino IDE

The following are the steps associated with connecting this device to Arduino:

1. The first step in accessing the device is to download the appropriate library. Here, you have a choice. You can use the library described in the *Connecting an accelerometer/gyro to Arduino* section, or you can download a library just for this device. The library supplied for the accelerometer/gyro is a more general library designed to communicate with many different I2C devices. The library for this device supports only this device. If you want to download the library for this device, go to www.sainsmart.com/sainsmart-bmp085-digital-pressure-sensor-module-board.html and select the **Download Link** selection at the bottom of the link. This will download a .rar file that will include an example sketch. I personally prefer to use the I2C library version; it is more up to date, so I will follow that example here.

2. Open the example by navigating to **File | Examples | BMP085 | Examples | BMP085_basic**, as shown in the following screenshot:

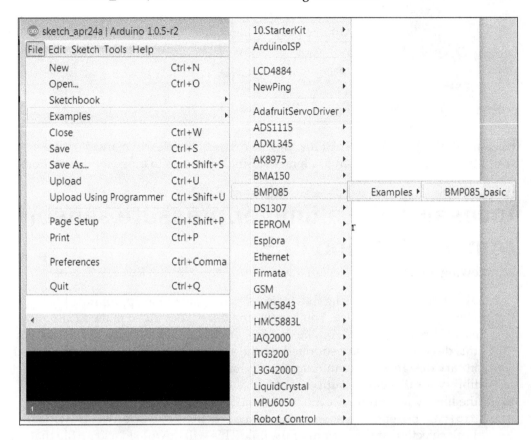

3. You should now set the Serial Monitor baud rate to 38400 if you haven't already done so, as this is the baud rate set by the example program. Now, you can upload the sketch of Arduino, and when you open the Serial Monitor, you should see something similar to the following screenshot:

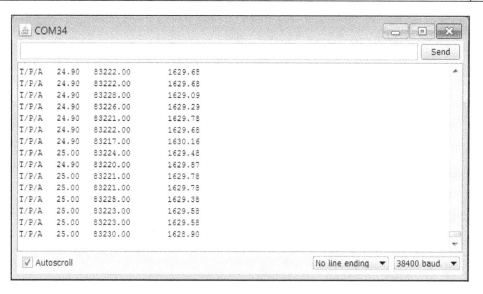

You can see not only the altitude, but the temperature and pressure as well. Now, this altitude is not an absolute value, but a relative one. It will change with a change in weather, as the barometric pressure is dependent on weather pattern changes. This particular reading is, therefore, really only useful when you want to measure the relative changes in altitude, for example, when you want to know how far your flying project has either gone up or done from a reference position.

Summary

There are many more sensors that we could have covered in this chapter, but hopefully, you have a feel of how you might be able to add them after following the instructions for these sensors. Your robot should now have lots of possible capabilities, but you are still tethered to the computer.

In the next chapter, you'll learn how to communicate with your robot wirelessly so that it won't need a cable to accept commands.

10
Going Truly Mobile – the Remote Control of Your Robot

Now that your robot is mobile and has several ways of sensing the outside world, you'll want to disconnect it from the tether cable that you have been using to communicate with it. In this chapter, you'll learn how to communicate wirelessly with your robot. Depending on your choice of method, you'll be able to communicate across the room or across a distance of up to a mile. Specifically, we'll cover the following topics:

- Connecting Arduino to a simple **radio frequency (RF)** transmitter/receiver pair
- Connecting Arduino to an XBee transmitter/receiver pair
- Connecting Arduino to a Bluetooth transmitter/receiver pair
- Connecting Arduino to a Wi-Fi network using a Wi-Fi shield

As your Arduino will now be remote, you'll need to power it with an external source. Your Arduino will need at least 250 mA, but you might want to consider providing 500 mA to 1 A based on your project. To supply this from a battery, you can use one of several different choices. One choice is a 4 AA battery pack, like the one used to power the DC motors on the wheeled robot in *Chapter 6, Controlling DC Motors*. Alternatively, you can also use an RC LiPo 2S battery, like the one you used to power the quadruped robot in *Chapter 7, Controlling Servos with Arduino*.

You can also use a simple USB battery, like the ones used to charge cell phones during an emergency, as shown in the following image:

Connecting a simple RF interface to Arduino

Let's start by connecting to Arduino with a simple RF interface. For this exercise, it will be easiest if you connect your development machine to Arduino with an RF interface and then connect to another Arduino with a similar RF transceiver. There are some very inexpensive modules available at online retailers such as ebay.com, but you will need to be a bit careful and watch what frequency your devices use, as they may violate your country's frequency usage rules. Each country regulates who can use what frequencies. For more information, visit www.wired.com/2010/09/ wireless-explainer/. For example, 433 MHz is fine for Europe, but can't be used in the US unless you have the proper amateur radio license. 915 MHz is available in the US but not in Europe. 2.4 GHz is fine in either case, so you might want to go with a transceiver that operates at 2.4 GHz.

The following is an image of a 2.4 GHz device, which is the nRF24L01+ 2.4 GHz wireless transceiver, available at many online retailers, including `amazon.com`:

You will want to purchase two of these devices. Initially, to try the example, connect each of the pair to your Arduino. You will also need to connect each device to a host computer so that you can monitor the **Serial Monitor** port. Eventually, when you have the system up and working, disconnect one of the devices from the host computer and connect it to a battery so that it can run without a host connection. To connect the devices to Arduino, connect to the pins on the back of the device. The following is an image of the connections on the back of the device:

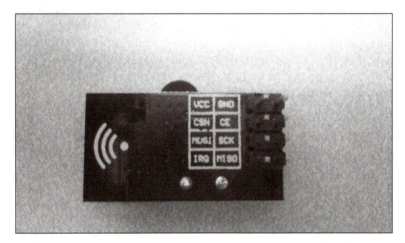

The following table shows the connections between the device and Arduino:

Arduino pin	Receiver pin
5 V	5 V
GND	GND
12	MISO
11	MOSI
13	SCK
8	CE
7	CSN

Connect the second Arduino in the same way as the first. Now, you are ready to access two Arduino IDEs, one for each of these two Arduinos.

Enabling a simple RF interface in the Arduino IDE

Let's start with Arduino that will receive the RF signal. You'll need to plug it into the host computer via a USB cable in order to upload a program. In order to debug both of these devices, you will also need two computers, one to run an Arduino IDE for both the transmit and receive device. You can also do this with a single computer and two USB ports (for more information on how to do this, visit `http://forum.arduino.cc/index.php?topic=407.0`). However, once you've created the program, you can disconnect the remote Arduino from the computer and power it from a battery. In this example, you'll use the example programs from the library to send data from the client (Arduino connected to the PC) to the server (the standalone Arduino) and then have it echo back.

As you did earlier, you'll first need to install the library. There are a couple of possible libraries, but the one that is the most full featured is the RF24 library, which is available at `https://github.com/maniacbug/RF24/`. To get the full library, select the **Download ZIP** button on the right side of the screen. Unzip the archive into a directory and then copy the directory to the `libraries` directory of your Arduino installation. You'll also need to rename this directory; I renamed mine `RF24`. To do this demo, you'll need two host computers, one for each RF device.

On both computers, open the Arduino IDE and bring up the server code by navigating to **File | Examples | RF24 | GettingStarted**, as shown in the following screenshot:

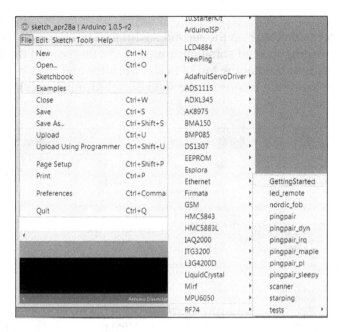

This Arduino will now have the code to configure the interface. When you bring up **Serial Monitor**, you should see something like the following screenshot:

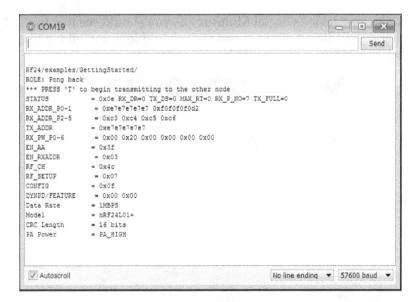

This shows the configuration of the first device. If you receive 0 for all values, you probably have your device connected incorrectly. Initially, this first device will be in receive mode, listening for a message, and when it receives one, it will send this message back to the sender.

Now, do the exact same thing on the second Arduino. The code you have will run and will also be waiting to send some information. On this second device, type the character T in the input field at the top of **Serial Monitor** and then hit **Send**. Now, you should begin to see the results on the send **Serial Monitor**, as shown in the following screenshot:

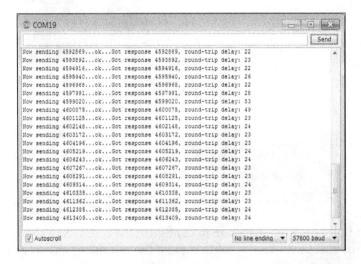

If you check the first device's **Serial Monitor** tab, you should see that it is now receiving the sending device's message. It should look something like the following screenshot:

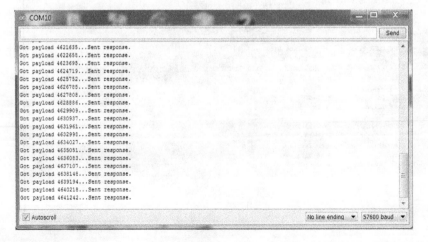

Now, you can disconnect the receive Arduino; it will retain this program and run it each time the unit is powered on. Connect this Arduino to a battery by plugging the battery GND and VCC to the GND and VIN pins on this receive Arduino. If you are using a cell phone's USB charger, you can connect it to the USB port on Arduino, as shown in the following image:

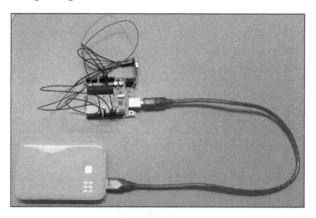

The LED on the receive Arduino should be flashing, indicating that the two Arduinos are communicating.

> To change the code to send a command byte, look for the following code that gets the milliseconds from the time function and sends it out to the other Arduino:
>
> ```
> // Take the time, and send it. This will block until
> complete
>     unsigned long time = millis();
>     printf("Now sending %lu...",time);
>     bool ok = radio.write( &time, sizeof(unsigned
> long));
> ```
>
> Now, change the code on the sending Arduino so that instead of sending the time, it sends a command byte that you define. Then, on the receive Arduino, look for the following code:
>
> ```
> // Grab the response, compare, and send to debugging
> spew
>     unsigned long got_time;
>     radio.read( &got_time, sizeof(unsigned long) );
>     // Spew it
>     printf("Got response %lu, round-trip delay: %lu\
> n\r",got_time,millis()-got_time);
> ```
>
> Finally, change this code to take the command byte that you defined and then trigger some action.

Connecting an XBee interface to Arduino

One of the most popular and well-documented ways of connecting to Arduino via an RF connection is to use an XBee device. This device uses a technology called ZigBee, and it is made for long-range wireless communications. These types of devices can work up to a range of 1 mile.

The ZigBee standard is built upon the IEEE 802.15.4 standard, a standard that was created to allow a set of devices to communicate with each other to enable low data rate coordination of multiple devices.

The other standard that you might hear as you try to purchase or use devices like these is XBee. This is a specific company's implementation, Digi, of several different wireless standards with standard hardware modules that can connect in many different ways to different embedded systems. They make several devices that support ZigBee standard. The following image shows the type of device that supports ZigBee attached to a small XBee-specific shield that provides a USB port:

The advantage of using this device is that it is configured to make it very easy to create and manage a simple link between two XBee series 1 devices. To make this work, you'll need the following four items:

- Make sure you have two XBee devices that support ZigBee series #1.
- You'll also need to purchase a small XBee-specific shield that provides a USB port connection to one of the two devices. This will provide communication from a host computer.

- You'll also need to buy a shield that plugs into your Arduino so that you can interface with the XBee devices. The following is an image of the shield plugged into Arduino with the XBee device plugged in:

Now, let's start to configure your two devices to talk. You'll need to configure both devices by plugging them into your host computer. Plug one of the devices into the small XBee-specific USB shield and then connect the shield to your personal computer. Your computer should find the latest drivers for the device. You should see your device when you select the **Devices and Printers** selection from the **Start** menu, as shown in the following screenshot:

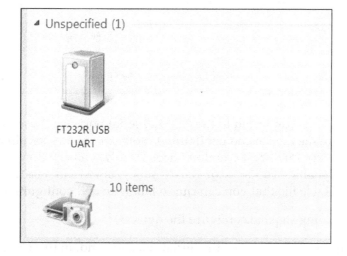

The device is now available to communicate via the IEEE 802.15.4 wireless interface. We could set up a full ZigBee-compliant network, but we're just going to communicate from one device to another directly. So, we'll just use the device as a serial port connection. Double-click on the device and then select the **Hardware** tab; you should see the following screenshot:

Note that the device is connected to the **COM20** serial port. We'll use this to communicate with the device and configure it. You can use any terminal emulator program; I like to use PuTTY. If you don't have PuTTY, you can download it from `www.chiark.greenend.org.uk/~sgtatham/putty/download.html`. This will provide an executable file that you can run to talk with and configure the devices.

Perform the following steps to configure the device:

1. Open up PuTTY and select the **Serial** selection and, in this case, the **COM20** port. The following screenshot shows you how to fill in the PuTTY window:

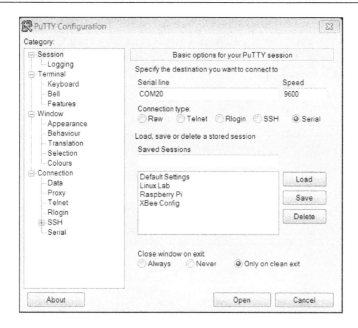

2. Configure the terminal window and set the following parameters:

- ° **Speed (baud)** as **9600**
- ° **Data bits** as 8
- ° **Stop bit** as 1
- ° **Parity** as **None**

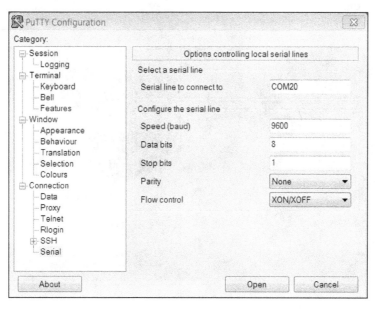

3. Make sure that you also select **Force on** in the **Local echo** option and check the **Implicit CR in every LF** and **Implicit LF in every CR** checkboxes (available under the **Terminal** tab in the **Category** selection), as shown in the following screenshot:

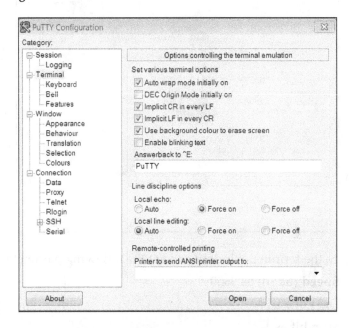

4. Connect to the device by selecting **Open**.
5. Enter the following commands to the device through the terminal window:

The OK response comes back from the device as you enter each command. The first device is now configured. Remove it from the small XBee-specific shield and plug it into the Arduino XBee shield.

Now, plug the second device into the small XBee shield and then plug it into the PC. Note that it might choose a different COM port; go to the **Devices and Printers** selection, double-click on the device, and select the **Hardware** tab to find the COM port. Follow the same steps to configure the second device, except that there are two changes. The ATMY value will be 2, and the ATDL value will be 1. The following screenshot shows the terminal window for these commands:

The two devices are now ready to communicate.

Enabling an XBee interface in the Arduino IDE

Let's first set up the Arduino IDE for XBee that will be connected to your Arduino. Once you have connected all the shields to your Arduino, simply connect your Arduino with the USB cable to one of the computers. Bring up the Arduino IDE and then type in the following code into the sketch window:

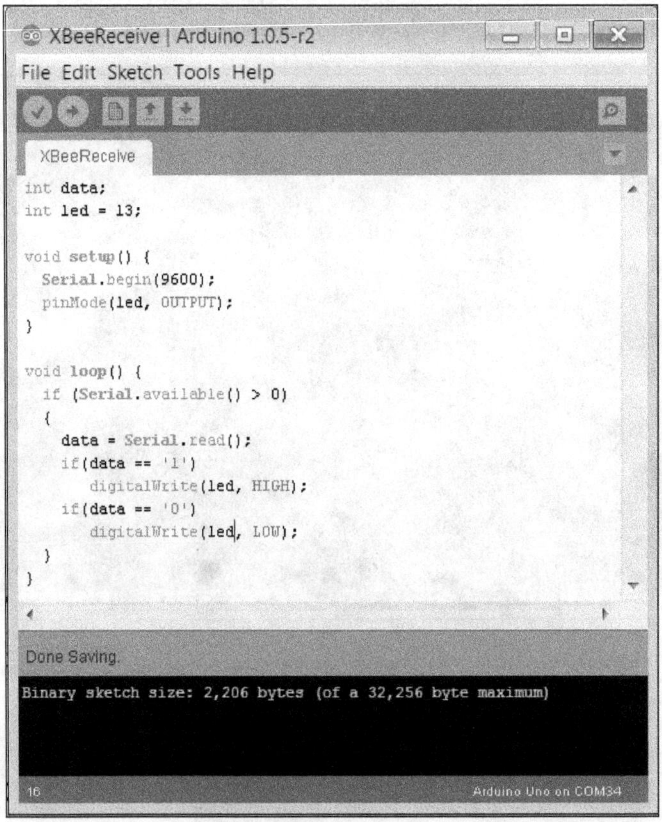
XBeeReceive | Arduino 1.0.5-r2
File Edit Sketch Tools Help
XBeeReceive
int data;
int led = 13;
void setup() {
Serial.begin(9600);
pinMode(led, OUTPUT);
}
void loop() {
if (Serial.available() > 0)
{
data = Serial.read();
if(data == '1')
digitalWrite(led, HIGH);
if(data == '0')
digitalWrite(led, LOW);
}
}
Done Saving.
Binary sketch size: 2,206 bytes (of a 32,256 byte maximum)
16
Arduino Uno on COM34

This sketch is quite simple; you can turn on the on-board LED with remote commands, 1 to turn it on and 0 to turn it off. Once you have compiled and uploaded this code, disconnect the USB cable from the computer. You'll need to physically change a switch setting on the wireless shield so that the device will now accept commands from your XBee controller. It is on the opposite end of the shield and looks like the following image:

When you are programming the device, you'll want this switch to be in the USB location. When you are ready to communicate with the device, you'll want to switch this to the MICRO setting. So, change it to the MICRO setting once your sketch has finished compiling and uploading to Arduino. Then, connect your Arduino to a battery.

Now, connect the other XBee device via the small Xbee-specific USB shield to the computer. Open PuTTY or any other terminal emulator window. Make sure that you set the terminal emulator data rate to **9800** baud. In PuTTY, your configuration will look like the following screenshot:

Now, open the terminal window. You should now be able to type 1 and the LED on the remote Arduino will turn on. Typing 0 should turn off the LED. Your PuTTY window should look like the following screenshot if you select **Force on** in the **Local echo** option and if the **Implicit CR in every LF** and **Implicit LF in every CR** options are checked:

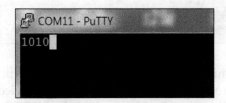

Now, if your system is not working, there are a couple of ways to try and determine what is going wrong. First and foremost, make sure Arduino is turned on and is executing the correct code. Second, check to see that characters are being typed in the PuTTY window. Third, check the baud rate of the PuTTY window. If this is too high, you will see characters come through the system, but they will not be interpreted correctly on Arduino.

Connecting a Bluetooth shield to Arduino

Another way of communicating wirelessly with Arduino is through a Bluetooth link. Bluetooth is a standard communications protocol that also works at 2.4 GHz. To read more about the Bluetooth protocol, visit http://www.bluetooth.com/Pages/Fast-Facts.aspx. There are several possible ways to connect your Arduino using Bluetooth, but the most reliable one is a Bluetooth shield, which is available at www.adafruit.com. The following is an image of the shield:

Unfortunately, you'll need to solder header pins onto the shield to mount it on your Arduino, but then, you'll need no additional connections. You'll also need a USB module if you want to communicate with your PC. The following is an image of an adapter that is also available at www.adafruit.com:

The learn.adafruit.com/introducing-bluefruit-ez-link/overview website will lead you through the details of how to get the shield up and working, paired with your Bluetooth dongle, and communicating with your other Bluetooth devices.

Connecting a Wi-Fi shield to Arduino

The final method you might consider to connect your Arduino wirelessly is with a wireless LAN shield. I will not cover Wi-Fi in detail, but rather just show you how to connect to Wi-Fi and point you in the general direction. Wi-Fi is clearly the most complex of the different ways to communicate, but it is a very common wireless communication tool used today. To know more about Wi-Fi, visit www.squidoo. com/what-is-wifi or www.radio-electronics.com/info/wireless/wi-fi/ ieee-802-11-standards-tutorial.php.

In order to connect to a wireless network, you'll need a Wi-Fi shield. The following is an image of the standard Arduino Wi-Fi shield:

Place the shield onto the Arduino Uno and you are ready to connect to a wireless network.

Enabling the Wi-Fi shield in the Arduino IDE

Now that the shield is attached, you can access the standard library examples for Wi-Fi. Navigate to **Examples | WiFi** and you'll see a number of useful example programs, as shown in the following screenshot:

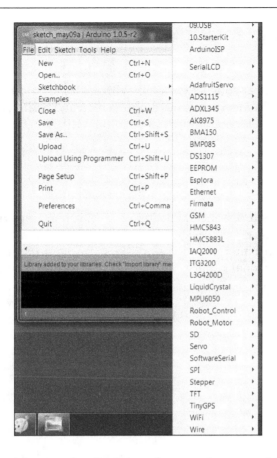

These are all very useful examples. Just to make sure that your shield works, you can select **ScanNetworks**. Run this program and open **Serial Monitor**. This program scans for available networks and should show a set of networks that are possible to connect to.

However, if you want to configure your Arduino as a Wi-Fi web server, you can access it via the Internet and get or send information to your Arduino via the Wi-Fi network. An excellent example to get you started is **SimpleWebServerWiFi**. Here, you enter your SSID and password and you can turn on an LED. I would suggest that you change the LED to pin 13, and you can then turn on and off the on-board LED via the instructions at the top of the file.

Connecting a GSM/GPRS shield to Arduino

There is one more way to connect remotely with Arduino, and this is via a GSM/GPRS shield. You'll also need access to a phone plan and a SIM card. I will not cover this in this chapter, so for more information, visit `arduino.cc/en/Guide/ArduinoGSMShield`.

Summary

As you now know, there are several useful ways of connecting wirelessly with your Arduino. You can choose a simple, inexpensive RF interface, a long-range XBee interface, or a standard interface such as Wi-Fi. Now, your robot can go untethered, needing only an occasional battery charge to keep it up and running.

In the next chapter, you'll learn how to connect a GPS device to your Arduino so that you can find out where you are and plan your next move.

11
Using a GPS Device with Arduino

You've got quite a set of tools now to build amazing robots. One part that is not yet covered, however, is giving your robot an idea of where it is in the world. This is particularly useful for autonomous robots that might have to travel long distances. Keeping track of its location would be useful, so you can not only know where your robot is, but also plan where it should go. In this chapter, you'll learn the following:

- How to connect a GPS device with Arduino using the I2C bus
- How to connect GPS capability using an Arduino shield

Let's get started with a brief GPS tutorial.

GPS tutorial

The **Global Positioning System (GPS)** is a system of satellites that transmits signals. GPS devices use these signals to calculate a position. There are a total of 24 satellites that transmit signals all around the earth at any given moment, but your device can only see the signal from a much smaller set of satellites.

Each of these satellites transmits a very accurate time signal that your device can receive and interpret. It receives the time signal from each of these satellites, and then, based on the delay (the time it takes the signal to reach the device), it calculates the receiver's position using a technique called triangulation.

The following two diagrams illustrate how the device uses the delay differences from three satellites to calculate its position:

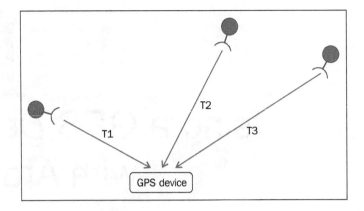

The GPS device is able to detect the three signals and the time delays associated with receiving these signals.

 Time delay refers to the time difference between the travel time of each of these three signals.

In the following diagram, the device is at a different location, and the time delays associated with the three signals have changed:

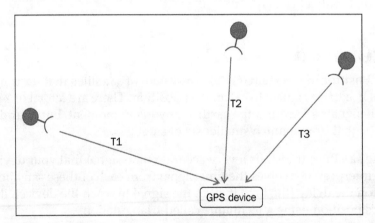

The time delays of the signals **T1**, **T2**, and **T3** can provide the GPS with an absolute position using a mathematical process called triangulation. Triangulation works like this: since the position of the satellites is known, the amount of time that the signal takes to reach the GPS device is also a measure of the distance between that satellite and the GPS device. To simplify, let's show an example in two dimensions. If the GPS device knows the value of the distance to one satellite based on the amount of time delay, you can draw a circle around the satellite at that distance and know that your GPS device is on that sphere, as shown in the following diagram:

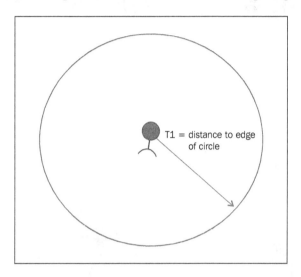

If you have two satellite signals and know the distance between the two, you can draw two circles as shown in the following diagram:

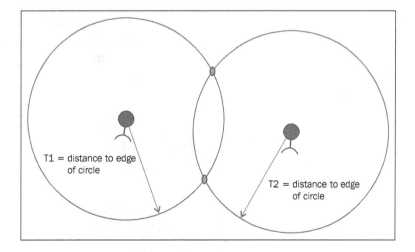

However, since you know that you can only be at points on the circle, you must be at one of the two points that are on both circles. Adding an additional satellite would eliminate one of these two points, thus providing you with an exact location. You need more satellites if you are going to do this in all three dimensions.

Now that you know how a GPS device works, let's connect one to Arduino.

Connecting a GPS device directly to Arduino

The first step is to find a suitable GPS device. There are many choices, but what you are looking for is a GPS device that can communicate via a bus that is available on Arduino. One possible device is VPN1513 GPS Receiver w/ Antenna, marketed by Parallax and available on their online store, `www.parallax.com`. The following is an image of the device:

Fortunately, this unit comes with its very own antenna, and you'll connect this to the RF (gold) connector on the board. This particular device interfaces using the I2C interface, one that your Arduino supports. In order to connect the device, you connect the pins to the board. The following is an image of these pins:

You'll connect your Arduino using the following connections:

Arduino pin	GPS cable pin
5V	5V
GND	GND
4	TX
3	RX

Now that the two devices are connected, you can access the device via the Arduino IDE.

Accessing the GPS device from the Arduino IDE

Now that your device is connected, you'll want to access the information from it programmatically. To do this, perform the following steps:

1. Copy the libraries and example programs for Arduino from `www.parallax.com/downloads/vpn1513-gps-receiver-w-antenna-arduino-example-code`.

2. Install the **TinyGPS** library into the **libraries** directory of Arduino.

3. Then, open the **test_with_gps_device** example, as shown in the following screenshot:

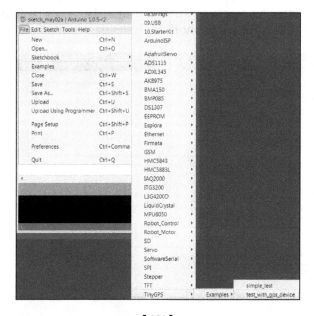

4. When you run that program and open the **Serial Monitor** tab, you should see the following display:

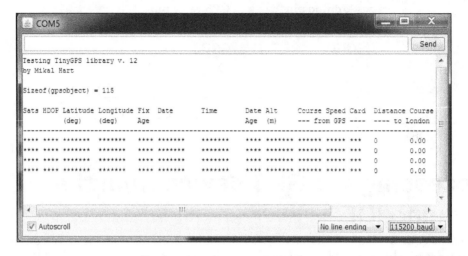

The information shows the status of the GPS receiver as well as the position, speed, time, date, and direction information. The status indication is the first column of data for each reading. This is important as it will tell you whether your device is reading enough satellites to get a valid positional calculation. This particular output indicates that even with your antenna, you are not getting a valid output. This means that your device cannot sense enough satellites to accurately calculate your current position.

Take the unit outside or at least near a window, and your device should be able to connect to enough satellites to get a value reading. Also, your display will change to the one seen in the following screenshot:

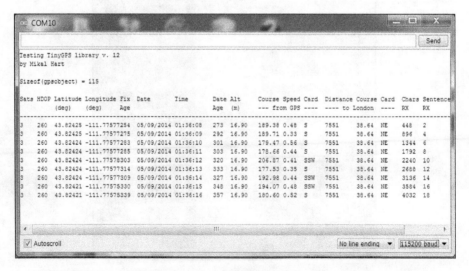

The following table offers an explanation of the important columns of data:

Column heading	Explanation
Stats	This is the number of satellites that the unit is receiving. This will need to be three for the GPS unit to get a valid position.
Latitude	This is the current latitude reading.
Longitude	This is the current longitude reading.
Alt	This is the current altitude reading.
Course (from GPS)	This is the current course reading from the GPS.
Speed (from GPS)	This is the current speed reading from the GPS.

For more information on the TinyGPS library, the data it gets from the GPS, and the purpose of all of the columns, visit arduiniana.org/libraries/tinygps/.

Connecting a GPS shield to Arduino

Now that you have an idea of how to connect a GPS device through the I/O pins on Arduino, let's look at a different way to provide GPS information to Arduino, through a GPS shield. There are several shields available, including one from Dexter Industries that is available at many online retailers, such as www.amazon.com.

To connect to Arduino, simply push the shield on your Arduino device so that it looks like the following image:

You can use the pin labels to match the pins on Arduino. Now, it is securely on top of your Arduino device; let's look at how to access the device via the SW.

Accessing the GPS shield from the Arduino IDE

The GPS shield provides the hardware interface to the GPS device. Now, you can access the GPS data from inside the Arduino IDE. To do this, perform the following steps:

1. As with most devices, the first step is to download the appropriate libraries. For this device, you'll find the libraries at `www.dexterindustries.com/ manual/arduino-shields/gps-shield/` under the **Arduino GPS Shield Drivers (zip)** selection.

2. Unzip the dGPS file and copy the dGPS file folder to your Arduino's **libraries** directory. You'll also need to download another three examples from this page. These aren't really set up to put in the **Examples** directory of **dGPS** and open automatically using the **File | Examples** process, but you can simply open them by navigating to **File | Open command**.

3. Once you have the library installed, let's write a simple program that reads the values from the GPS device. Open the Arduino IDE and type in the following code:

4. Now, upload the preceding code to Arduino and then open **Serial Monitor**. You should see something like the following screenshot:

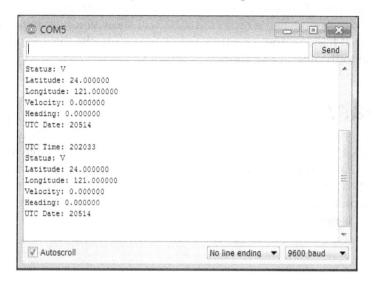

These are the GPS readings from the device. As noted in the previous section, **Status** tells you whether or not your device is locked to enough satellites. In this case, **V** indicates that our device is not. You may need to go outside a building to connect with enough satellites to get a valid reading. A valid reading would look like the following screenshot:

The library for this device is quite extensive, and you can get back much more than your position. In fact, *Example 2: Calculating GPS distance to destination, azimuth (angle of travel) to destination. (zip)* that you can download from www.dexterindustries. com/manual/arduino-shields/gps-shield/ will show you how to use the library to enter a desired latitude and longitude value and return the distance as well as the angle of travel to the desired location.

Summary

In this chapter, you've learned how to connect your robot to the GPS system. Now, your robot will have a sense of where it is. It should also be able to roll or walk, sense its surroundings, and even communicate with a remote computer. However, GPS is particularly useful when you build sailing or flying robots. In the upcoming chapters, you'll use these capabilities to build robots than can fly and even go under water.

12
Taking Your Robot to Sea

Now that you have the set of tools, let's build some amazing robots. Let's start by exploring robots that can go either in or under water. I won't cover every detail in this chapter, but I will discuss some additional capabilities that you'll need in order to complete these more advanced projects. In this chapter, you'll learn the following:

- How to build a sailing robot
- How to build a **remote operated vehicle (ROV)** using Arduino that can explore underwater

Let's start by sailing!

Building an automated sailing platform

Certainly, one of the most impressive ways to navigate the waters is in a sailing vessel. Let's start with an RC sailboat. These are available at many hobby stores, either retail or online. The following is an image of one such platform:

This sailboat is ready to sail via radio control. This means that it has two servos mounted inside: one to control the sail and the other to control the rudder. The following is an image of these two servos that are connected to the sail and rudder:

In order for your sailboat to sail itself, it will need several key capabilities. First, it should be able to control the servos; you'll use the techniques you learned in *Chapter 7, Controlling Servos with Arduino*, to move the rudder and trim the sails. You might want to add the GPS capability that you discovered in *Chapter 11, Using a GPS Device with Arduino*. You will want to control the system without a wired connection, so you can use the principles that you learned in *Chapter 10, Going Truly Mobile – the Remote Control of Your Robot*.

One additional item that you might want to add for a fully automated system is a wind sensor. The following is an image of a wind sensor. A fairly inexpensive one is available at www.moderndevice.com:

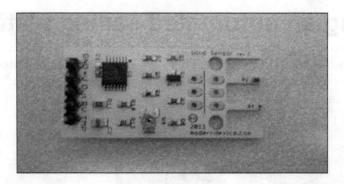

You can mount the wind sensor on the mast if you'd like; I used a small piece of heavy-duty tape and mounted it on the top of the mast, as shown in the following image:

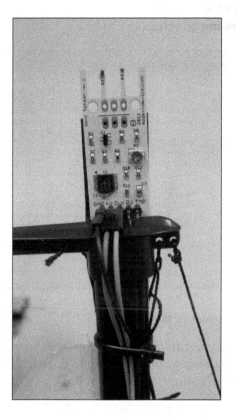

To add this to your system, you'll also need a way to take the analog input from the sensor and send it to Arduino. Notice that the device has three connections that you'll be using: GND, +V, and Out. Connect your Arduino to the wind sensor using the following connections:

Arduino pin	Wind sensor pin
5V	+V
GND	GND
A1	RV
A0	TMP

Accessing the device in a sketch is straightforward; in fact, the manufacturer has included an example sketch at `github.com/moderndevice/Wind_Sensor`. Unzip, open, and upload the `WindSensor` sketch. Then, open **Serial Port**, set the baud rate to **57600 baud**, and blow with your mouth on the sensor. You should see something like the following screenshot:

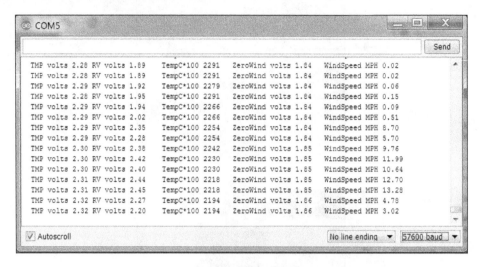

Now you have a way to measure the wind!

By the way, here is where you can take advantage of the stackable nature of the devices. The following is an image of my Arduino board, the Wireless SD shield with an XBee device, and the GPS shield, all connected:

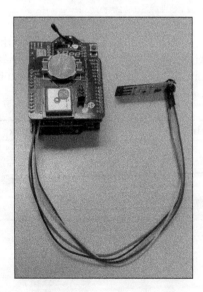

The wind sensor is connected to the holes available on the Wireless SD shield. You'll also need to add the servo control, but now, you have all the capabilities you need to build your Arduino-controlled sailing vessel. However, Arduino is not limited to just sailing above the water. Let's see how you can build a robot that can go under water.

Building an Arduino-powered underwater ROV

An ROV offers an entirely different way to use Arduino to explore a new world. This project is a bit different in two ways. First, there is quite a bit of mechanical work to do, and second, it is almost impossible to send wireless signals through water. So, you are going to use a tethered control line to give your robot direction.

Building an ROV

There are several possible approaches to building your ROV. Although controlled by a different processor, the mechanical design at openrov.com/page/openrov-2-0 is quite elegant, and you could certainly build the HW yourself and then integrate your Arduino. At openrov.com/page/open-rov-designs-1 is a simpler yet similar design that incorporates Arduino. Another design that is very different from the first one is available at www.instructables.com/id/Underwater-ROV/. Both could certainly use Arduino as the motor control.

My physical design is based more on the latter design that mostly uses plastic piping, as shown in the following image:

One of the most important components of your ROV is the clear plastic casing, as you need to be able to use a camera to see the world underwater. The following is an image of the one I used:

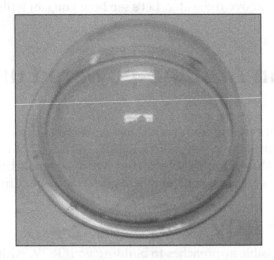

This came from a company called EZ Tops and can be ordered online at www.eztopsworldwide.com/smalldomes.htm. I put this on the other end of my ROV, assembled with a gasket and some small bolts. Whether you use a round design or a more traditional square design, you'll want a clear plastic so that you can get a good view of the underwater world.

Controlling brushless DC motors with Arduino

Whatever physical design you choose, you'll need to control the motors, and Arduino is well suited for this task. In this case, I chose fairly standard brushless DC motors and then fitted them with RC boat propellers. These motors work just fine underwater and are easy to control with RC **electronic speed controllers** (**ESCs**).

For this project, you'll need four brushless DC motors and four ESC controllers. You'll need to make sure that the ESCs will be able to control the motors to go both forward and backward. The following is an image of one such unit:

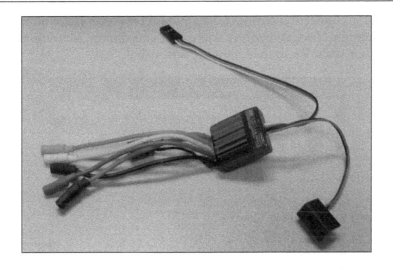

This particular unit is a Turnigy Trackstart 25A ESC, made normally for an RC car and available at many RC outlets, both retail and online. The connections on this unit are straightforward. The red and black wires with plugs go to an RC battery, in this case, a 2S 7.4 volt LiPo RC battery. The other three plugs go to the motor. This particular ESC comes with a switch; you won't use it in this particular project. The last connection is a three-wire connector, similar to a servo connection. You'll connect this to Arduino. The following diagram shows the connections:

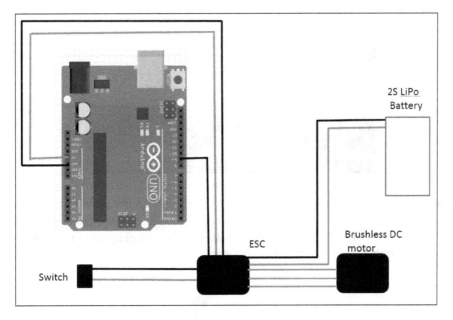

For details on the connection between the ESC and brushless DC motor, check your ESC documentation. Now that you've connected your motor, a simple sketch to control the motor is shown in the following screenshot:

Note that you will use the servo control process to control the speed of your motor. With these ESCs, 0 will be full speed backward, 180 will be full speed forward, and 90 will stop the motor. The setup() function sets the initial speed to 90, just so that your motors won't take off right from the start.

Now, open the **Serial Monitor** tab and enter a `speed` value close to `90`; you'll see the following screenshot:

The motor should spin both forward and backward. You don't necessarily need to do so, but ESCs can also be programmed. I won't cover that in this chapter; check your ESC documentation for the additional HW required. The ESC may also want to be calibrated. The procedure will change based on your particular ESC, but the basic steps are as follows:

1. Disconnect your motor.

2. Power up the ESC by applying maximum forward throttle; in this case, `speed` = `180`.

3. You'll hear a tone and some beeps. Then, after a few seconds, you will hear a confirmation tone, and the LED will blink a few times. This means that the ESC has calibrated maximum throttle.

4. Now, apply minimum throttle, or `speed` = `0`. The unit should emit some tones, and the LED will blink. Now, minimum throttle has been calibrated.

5. Now, go to the middle throttle, or `speed` = `90` in this case, and the unit will emit some tones and blink. Your unit is now calibrated.

You'll use four of the digital I/O pins, one for each motor. Controlling the speed and direction of each of these motors will allow you to move your ROV forward, backward, up, and down, as well as turn your ROV. How much speed you apply will depend on both the size of your ROV and the size of your motors.

Now, your ROV is maneuverable. To complete your ROV project, you'll need two additional capabilities. The first is a LAN shield for your Arduino so that you can control and communicate with your ROV via the LAN cable that will run from your ROV to the surface. The second is a way to see underwater. Let's tackle the control problem first.

Connecting a LAN shield to Arduino

The ROV will be controlled from a computer on the surface through a very long LAN cable. This will require you to add LAN capability to your Arduino, so you will need to add a LAN shield to your project. There are several shields available; the following is an image of a standard Arduino LAN shield available at `arduino.cc`:

When you have obtained the shield, attach it to the top of your Arduino. Now, you can open the Arduino IDE, and the first example you'll use is a simple web page access of data. To do this, open the **WebServer** example by navigating to **File | Examples | Ethernet | WebServer**, as shown in the following screenshot:

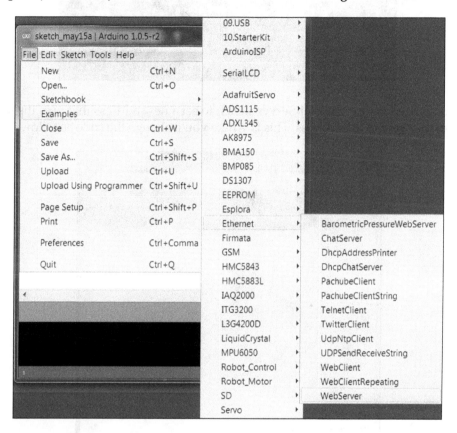

Using a web server will allow you to access your Arduino via the LAN cable that will be connected to your ROV from a web browser on a computer at the surface. To connect with the device, you'll need to set the appropriate address for the Arduino web page.

To do this, run `ipconfig` from the command prompt (under the **Accessories** folder) on your computer. When you run this, you should see something like the following screenshot:

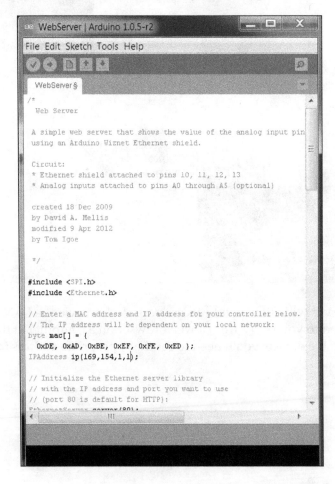

You'll now need to edit the **WebServer** sketch to set a new address that uses the same first two numbers in the address. This is where you'll change the code as follows:

Open the **Serial Monitor** tab and you should see the following screenshot:

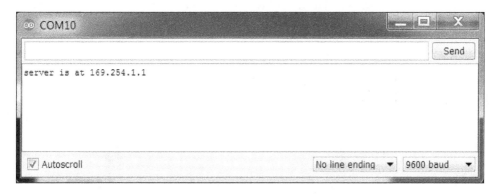

Now, open a web page and type in the IP address you set in the sketch, and you should see the following screenshot:

You'll need two additional capabilities to control your ROV. The first is the ability to use the LAN connection to control your motors. You can do this through a web page interface.

The tutorials at `startingelectronics.com/tutorials/arduino/ethernet-shield-web-server-tutorial/` and `www.instructables.com/id/Arduino-Ethernet-Shield-Tutorial/` provide lots of details on how to access your Arduino via a web page, and `www.power7.net/arduinoethernet.html` shows how to incorporate even more examples of control using a web page.

In this example, you'll use some simple code to control the speed of the four motors: two to move the ROV forward and backward and two to move the ROV up and down. The following screenshot shows the first part of the Arduino sketch, the initialization part:

```
#include <SPI.h>
#include <Ethernet.h>

byte mac[] = { 0xDE, 0xAD, 0xBE, 0xEF, 0xFE, 0xED };
byte ip[] = { 169,254,1,1 };

const int MAX_PAGENAME_LEN = 8;
char buffer[MAX_PAGENAME_LEN+1];

EthernetServer server(80);

#include <Servo.h>
Servo myservo1;
int servo1 = 9;
Servo myservo2;
int servo2 = 10;
Servo myservo3;
int servo3 = 11;
Servo myservo4;
int servo4 = 12;

void setup()
{
  Serial.begin(9600);
  myservo1.attach(servo1);
  myservo2.attach(servo2);
  myservo3.attach(servo3);
  myservo4.attach(servo4);
  Ethernet.begin(mac, ip);
  server.begin();
  Serial.println("Initialization done");
  delay(2000);
}
```

This sets up the web configuration and declares all of your servos to control the four motors. The next part is the web server part of the code in the `loop()` function, as shown in the following screenshot:

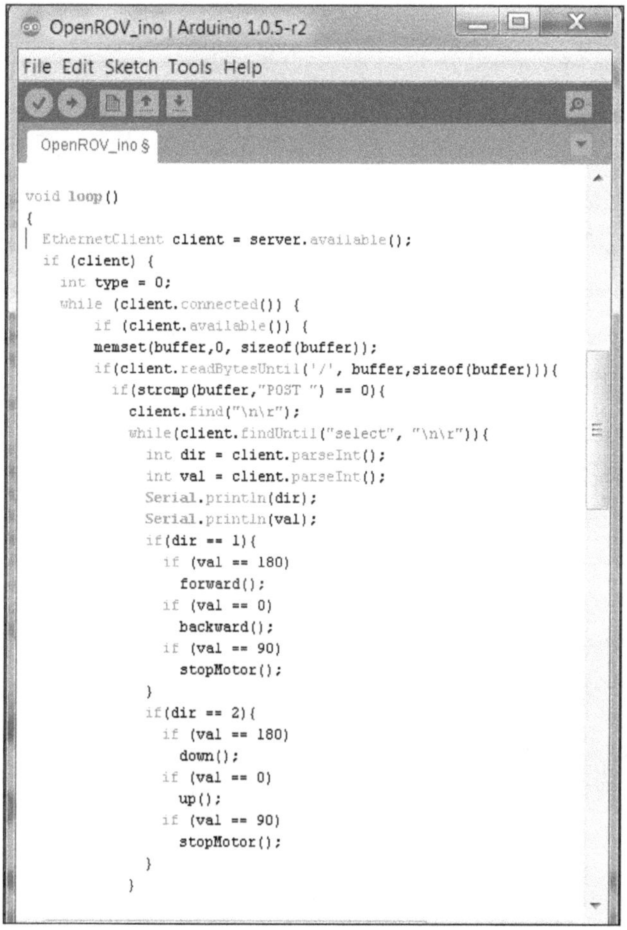
OpenROV_ino | Arduino 1.0.5-r2
File Edit Sketch Tools Help
OpenROV_ino §
void loop()
{
EthernetClient client = server.available();
if (client) {
int type = 0;
while (client.connected()) {
if (client.available()) {
memset(buffer,0, sizeof(buffer));
if(client.readBytesUntil('/', buffer,sizeof(buffer))){
if(strcmp(buffer,"POST ") == 0){
client.find("\n\r");
while(client.findUntil("select", "\n\r")){
int dir = client.parseInt();
int val = client.parseInt();
Serial.println(dir);
Serial.println(val);
if(dir == 1){
if (val == 180)
forward();
if (val == 0)
backward();
if (val == 90)
stopMotor();
}
if(dir == 2){
if (val == 180)
down();
if (val == 0)
up();
if (val == 90)
stopMotor();
}
}

This part parses the input from the web page and calls the functions that cause your ROV to go forward, backward, up, down, or stop. The final part of the loop creates these controls, as shown in the following screenshot:

```
                }
                sendHeader(client,"ROV Example");
                client.println("<h2><font color=#f6a343>ROV - Motor Control</h2>");
                client.print(
                "<form action='/' method='POST'><p><input type='hidden' name='select1'");
                client.println(" value='180'><input type='submit' value='Forward'/></form>");
                client.print(
                "<form action='/' method='POST'><p><input type='hidden' name='select1'");
                client.print(" value='0'><input type='submit' value='Back'/></form>");
                client.print(
                "<form action='/' method='POST'><p><input type='hidden' name='select1'");
                client.print(" value='90'><input type='submit' value='Stop'/></form>");
                client.print(
                "<form action='/' method='POST'><p><input type='hidden' name='select2'");
                client.println(" value='0'><input type='submit' value='Up'/></form>");
                client.print(
                "<form action='/' method='POST'><p><input type='hidden' name='select2'");
                client.print(" value='180'><input type='submit' value='Down'/></form>");
                client.print(
                "<form action='/' method='POST'><p><input type='hidden' name='select2'");
                client.print(" value='90'><input type='submit' value='Stop'/></form>");

                client.println("</body></html>");

                client.stop();
            }
        }
    }

    delay(1000);
    client.stop();
    }
}
```

The final part of the sketch is a function to create the header for the web page and the functions to control the motor, as shown in the following screenshot:

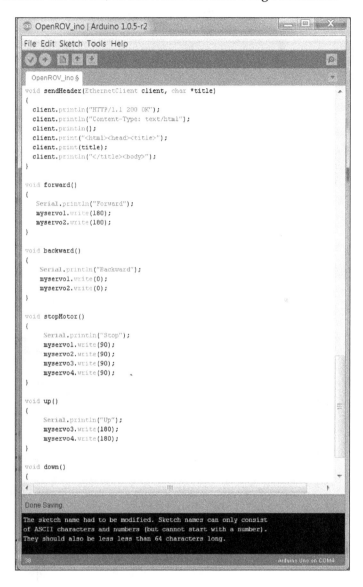

You can now run this sketch by first opening the **Serial Monitor** tab and then opening a web page and typing the address at the top of the web page. You should then see the following interface to control the ROV:

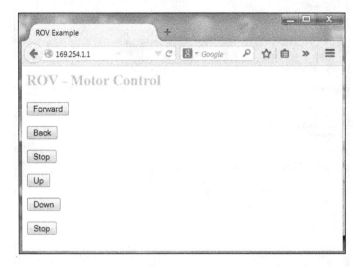

In the **Serial Monitor** tab, you should see the commands come through, as shown in the following screenshot:

If your motors are connected to the control pins, as covered earlier in the chapter, your motors should be ready to drive your ROV up, down, backward, forward, or stop all motors. You may have to adjust the settings based on the direction of your motors' spin and also the desired speed.

Accessing a camera for your project

Now that you have established connection via a LAN connection, the second capability you'll need is to access a camera to see where you are going. One of the most significant questions is whether or not connecting a camera to Arduino will work in this application. There are several cameras that can be accessed either through a standard UART RX/TX or I2C interface. The following is an image of one such unit, available from RadioShack:

There are two ways to connect the camera. The first is through a UART interface, the other is through an I2C interface. Connecting the camera and getting it to write the images to the SD card interface is a bit daunting, but there is an example sketch available at www.radioshack.com. There is also a tutorial that looks promising at http://makezine.com/projects/crittergram-capture-cam/. Be forewarned that getting this to work is not easy; there is a significant amount of configuration required.

You will also find that the refresh rate on any Arduino-based camera system will be marginal at best. The challenge is that there is no high-speed bus between the camera and Arduino, and you'll be saving the pictures on the SD card for later transmission.

For this application, I chose a different solution: I purchased an IP camera that I could connect to the LAN cable. The following is an image of the unit:

I chose this particular camera because it is inexpensive, less expensive than camera shields available for Arduino, and its small size made it easy to mount on the ROV. With this particular unit, you can issue commands to turn it from side to side and up and down, and turn on LED lighting, which would make it a good choice for dark situations. If you go with this choice, you will have to add a switch to your ROV so that both the motor control and the camera can connect to the LAN cable from the surface.

Your surface computer will now have two web pages, one to access and control the camera and the web page you just created to control the motors. The following is an image of the motor control web page:

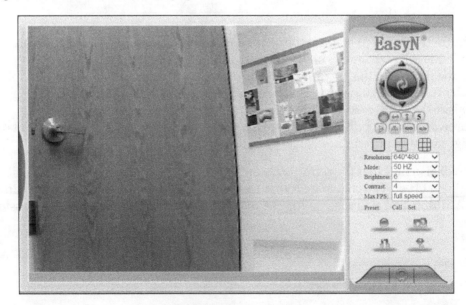

Note that you can change the direction of the camera right from the web page, and you can also turn on the lights. You're now ready to go underwater. Just a word of advice: be prepared to add significant weight to your ROV. I had to add 25 pounds of lead to mine to get it to do anything but bob on top of the surface!

Summary

In this chapter, you've tackled a sailing robot and a robot that can go underwater. You've learned how to add unusual sensors such as the wind sensor on the sailboat. You've also learned how to control a project via a LAN connection across a significant distance with the ROV project. In the next chapter, you'll move on to projects that can fly.

13
Robots That Can Fly

In this chapter, we'll cover robots that can fly. As with the last chapter, we won't cover every detail in this chapter, but we will again discuss how to bring all the different capabilities that we have covered to our new projects. We'll also discuss the additional capability that you will need. In this chapter, you'll learn the following:

- How to build an Arduino-operated RC airplane
- How to build an Arduino-operated quadcopter

Let's get started!

Building an Arduino-operated plane

At this point, you have all the tools you need to add Arduino to an RC-controlled airplane. So, let's tackle that project. You're going to add control so that you can control your RC plane from a phone, tablet, or any device with Bluetooth capability. Then, you'll learn how to add some of the additional sensors you've used in other projects, such as GPS, to make your RC plane even more intelligent by making it autonomous.

First, find an RC airplane. They are available at most RC hobby stores and online. I ordered this one from `amazon.com`:

You could use one of the many different makes and models of RC planes for this project, as long as they meet a few requirements. If you are new to RC airplanes and how they operate, you might first read about them at `www.instructables.com/ id/Beginners-Guide-to-Radio-Control-Airplanes/`. The first requirement for this project is that the plane must be RC controlled and the RC unit must control the servos and speed of the unit. The second requirement is that it should be large enough so that Arduino can fit on the plane without taking up too much room. As the programming required for this project is minimal, you can use a fairly small Arduino to control the plane. Finally, I chose a plane with a rear-facing propeller. We have found that many times, the plane will come down nose first, and having a rear-facing propeller helps the plane survive more crash landings. You will have several of those.

If this is your first project, you may want to order an RC airplane with simple controls, perhaps with two control surfaces and a speed control. These will often be referred to as 3 Channel RC airplanes.

The first step will be to locate your control servos, speed control, and the wires that are connected to them. In this particular airplane, the servos are integrated with the receiver, so you'll need to remove the entire board and replace it with two micro servos. A suitable micro servo is the HS-55 from Hitec, available at many hobby stores and most electronics online retailers.

I placed my micro servos using velcro, and they fit very nicely in the opening. The following image shows all the control connections for this particular RC airplane after replacing the servos:

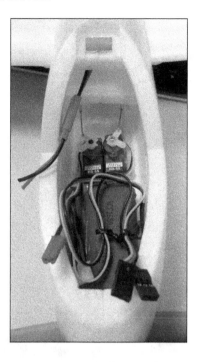

You'll need to connect the two servos, the red and black wires from the motor, and the red and black wires from the battery to your Arduino. The control signals you'll need to provide with your Arduino are the two servos for the control surfaces, and the DC motor that is attached to your propeller is the control for speed.

Now, you'll need to add your Arduino. You can certainly use one of the standard Arduinos that you've used in the previous projects, but there are also some special-purpose Arduinos that are excellent for this particular application. One in particular is small and comes with wireless communication; it is called the RFduino.

This device uses Bluetooth technology to communicate with other devices. It is available at several online electronics retailers. The following is an image of the unit:

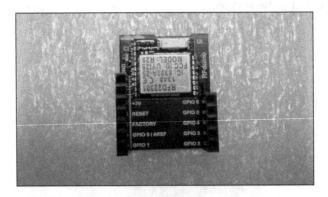

You'll also need a couple of the shields that are available for the RFduino, in particular, the USB development shield, the battery shield, and the servo control shield. The following is an image of all three:

Each shield performs an important function, as follows:

- **USB development shield**: This will allow you to develop on the RFduino platform using a standard computer
- **Battery shield**: This will supply the power when you are flying your airplane
- **Servo Control shield**: This will interface with the RC plane servos and speed controller

So, let's start building.

First, plug the RFduino into the USB shield, and then plug the servo control shield into the RFduino. Now, plug the USB into the USB port of your computer. Then, follow the instructions at `www.rfduino.com/wp-content/uploads/2014/04/RFduino.Quick_.Start_.Guide_.pdf` to get the entire system up and connected. You'll need to download a beta version of the Arduino IDE, Version 1.5; however, you may want to keep the current released version as well. Just make sure you remember which version is in which location.

For your application, let's start by opening a simple example program that allows the RFduino to control the servos. To do this, navigate to **Examples** | **RFduinoBLE** | **Servo** as shown in the following screenshot:

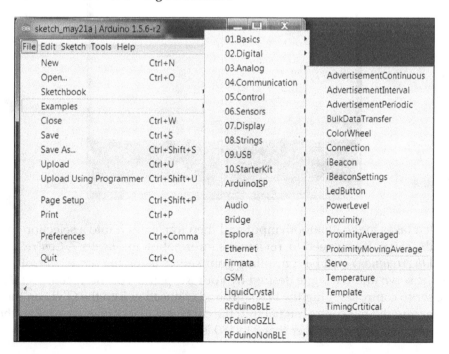

The code is very simple, and it is as follows:

The sketch takes in the Bluetooth input and then translates it into a selection to control the servo. If you need to, review the information in *Chapter 7, Controlling Servos with Arduino*. You'll be controlling your servos using the servo controller, setting the servo and the angle desired by your RC plane. For the speed, you'll also use the servo controller; plug the black ground connection into the GND on the servo controller and the red control signal into the control signal connector spot on the servo controller. Just remember that 0 to 180 is the speed control value.

You'll now need an application on your tablet or phone to control the RFduino over the Bluetooth link. If you are adventurous enough to develop your own application, visit `http://www.rfduino.com/download-rfduino-library/` for example programs. Most of these example programs are already created and on the iPhone app page. To test your control, you can download these apps and run them. The RFduino servo control app should allow you to control your servos and speed so that you can control your plane remotely.

The RFduino team has not yet created an Android app, but if you have an Android device, there are already several Android BT Arduino control applications on the Google Play store that can be of use. For example, the Arduino BT Joystick PRO app can be used to communicate with your device. You'll need to translate the Bluetooth commands as they come in from the Bluetooth interface and then send control signals to the various control surfaces of your airplane, but this will give you more control over your airplane.

This will take a bit of Android development programming, and you'll need to make changes so that the up, down, left, and right arrows adjust the control surfaces of your airplane appropriately. Also, be careful; Bluetooth does have a limited range. So, don't get much more than 50 meters from your plane, or it might just fly away.

Once you have your plane flying, you can add the digital compass discussed in *Chapter 9, Even More Useful Sensors*. If you know direction and calibrate your speed, your Arduino can even have a sense of where it is. You could even, in the absence of any control commands from the Bluetooth interface, fly your airplane in circles.

Even more interesting would be to add the accelerometer/gyro capability from the same chapter. Connecting and calibrating the device would give your Arduino information on when the airplane was flying level or when it is going up or down or rolling on its side. You can then use your controls to force the plane back into the desired position. The specifics on this type of control are too complex to detail in this chapter, so for more information, visit `www.instructables.com/id/Intro-to-Model-Airplane-Autopilot/` and `hacknmod.com/hack/make-a-uav-spyplane-using-the-arduino/`.

Building a quadcopter platform

Quadcopters are a unique subset of flying platforms that have become very popular in the last few years. They are a flying platform that utilize the same vertical lift concept as helicopters; however, they employ not one but four motor/propeller combinations to provide an enhanced level of stability. The following is an image of such a platform:

The quadcopter has two sets of counter-rotating propellers, which simply means that two of the propellers rotate clockwise and the other two rotate counter-clockwise to provide thrust in the same direction. This provides a platform that is inherently stable. Controlling the thrust of all four motors allows you to change the pitch, roll, and yaw of the device. The following is an image that may be helpful:

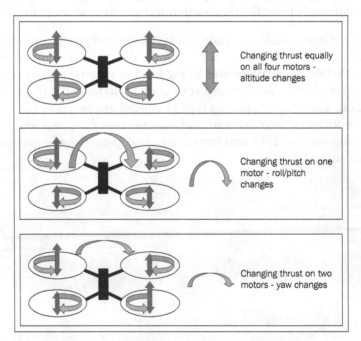

As you can see, controlling the relative speeds of the four motors allows you to control the various ways in which the device can change position. To move forward, or really in any direction, we would combine a change in roll/pitch with a change in thrust so that instead of going up, the device would move forward, as shown in the following diagram:

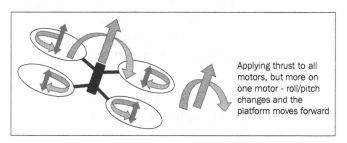

Applying thrust to all motors, but more on one motor - roll/pitch changes and the platform moves forward

In a perfect world, you might know exactly how much control signal to apply to get a certain change in the roll/pitch/yaw or altitude of your quadcopter, as you know the components you used to build your quadcopter. However, there are simply too many aspects of your device that can vary to know this well enough to rely on a fixed set of signals. Instead, this platform uses a series of measurements of its position, pitch/roll/yaw, and altitude and then adjusts the control signals to the motors to achieve the desired result. We call this feedback control. The following is a diagram of a feedback system:

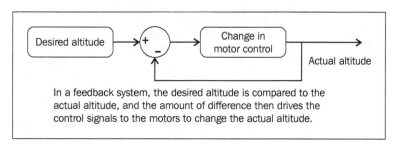

In a feedback system, the desired altitude is compared to the actual altitude, and the amount of difference then drives the control signals to the motors to change the actual altitude.

As you can see, if your quadcopter is too low, the difference between the desired altitude and the actual altitude will be positive, and the motor control will increase the voltage to the motors, thus increasing the altitude. If the quadcopter is too high, the difference between the desired altitude and the actual altitude will be negative, and the motor control will decrease the voltage to the motors, thus decreasing the altitude. If the desired altitude and the actual altitude are equal, the difference between the two will be zero, and the motor control will be held at its current value. Thus, the system stabilizes even if the components aren't perfect or if a wind comes along and blows the quadcopter up or down.

One application of Arduino in this type of robotic project is to actually coordinate the measurement and control of the quadcopter's pitch/roll/yaw and altitude. To accomplish this task, there are two approaches. First, configure Arduino and hook up the gyroscope, altimeter, GPS, and magnetic direction-finding sensors, and code all of the control algorithms yourself. The detail for all of this is beyond the scope of this book, but there are several excellent sites that support this. They can be found at `aeroquad.com/content.php?s=f2b480cc710c1d5611dd3dbe254cee9c` and `jbquad.blogspot.com/2013/02/intro-to-project-quadcopter.html`. You can also visit `github.com/baselsw/BlueCopter`, which provides a sketch that you could start with.

The second and certainly the easier one of the two approaches is to choose ArduPilot as a flight-control system; Arduino designed it specifically for this application. The following is an image of this unit:

This flight system uses a flight version of Arduino to do the low-level feedback control we talked about earlier. The advantage to this system is that you won't need to create and debug lots of Arduino kit.

Either way, you'll need to build a quadcopter:

- Purchase a kit and construct it yourself
- Purchase a quadcopter that is already assembled

There are a number of assembled quadcopters available that use the ArduPilot flight controller. One place to start is at `ArduPilot.com`. This will give you some information on the flight controller, and the store has several quadcopters that are already assembled. If you are thinking that assembling a kit is the right approach, try `www.unmannedtechshop.co.uk/multi-rotor.html` or `www.buildyourowndrone.co.uk/ArduCopter-Kits-s/33.htm`, as each of these not only sell assembled quadcopters, but kits as well.

If you'd like to assemble your own kit, there are several good tutorials about choosing all the right parts and assembling your quadcopter. Visit `blog.tkjelectronics.dk/2012/03/quadcopters-how-to-get-started`, `blog.oscarliang.net/build-a-quadcopter-beginners-tutorial-1/` and `http://www.arducopter.co.uk/what-do-i-need.html`.

All of these links have excellent instructions. The following is an image of a quadcopter that we built; it uses the ArduPilot:

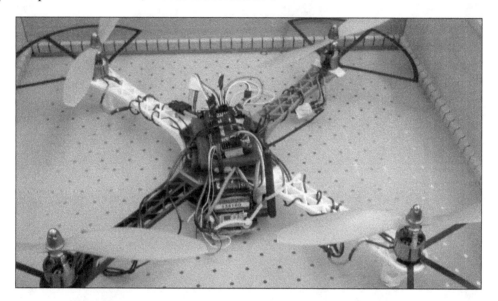

No matter which path you choose, another excellent source for information is `http://code.google.com/p/arducopter`. This gives you some information on how the ArduPilot works and also talks about Mission Planner, the open source control SW that will be used to control the ArduPilot on your quadcopter. This SW runs on your PC and communicates with the quadcopter in one of two ways: either directly through a USB connection or through a radio connection.

The first step in working in this space is to build your quadcopter and get it working with an RC radio. When you allow Arduino to control it later, you may still want to have the RC radio handy, just in case things don't go quite as planned.

When the quadcopter is flying well based on your ability to control it using the RC radio, you should then begin to use the ArduPilot in the autopilot mode. To do this, download the Mission Planner SW from `ArduPilot.com/downloads`. You can then run the SW, and you should see something like the following screenshot:

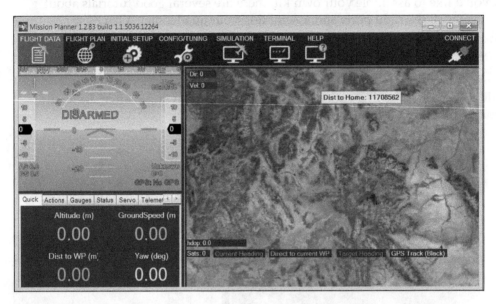

You can then connect your ArduPilot to the SW and click on the **CONNECT** button in the upper-right corner of the screen. You should then see something like the following screenshot:

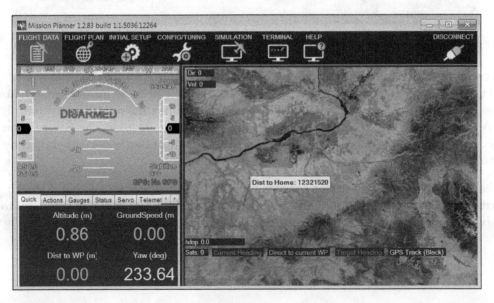

We will not walk you through how to use the SW to plan an automated flight path; there is plenty of documentation for that on the `ArduPilot.com` website. If you connect a GPS device to the unit, you can even ask your quadcopter to fly to specific points.

Summary

In this chapter, you learned how to build an Arduino-controlled airplane. You also learned how to build an Arduino-controlled quadcopter. Now, your robot can sail, go underwater, and even fly. In the next chapter, I'll introduce you to a number of smaller projects that can be done quickly and very inexpensively but produce some amazing results.

14
Small Projects with Arduino

We've covered all kinds of mobile robots. In this chapter, for a change of pace, you'll learn how to build small Arduino-based projects. By small, I mean not only small in size, but small in effort. In this chapter, you'll learn the following topics:

- How to modify a small, walking robot by adding Arduino
- How to build wearable projects that can add style and flair to your robot

First, let's build some really small robots with Arduino.

Small robots and Arduino

We covered some large robots in the earlier chapters; in this section, you'll build much smaller robots. You can build these small robots from scratch, but I've found that it is much easier and less expensive to take toy robots, which provide the basic capabilities, and add Arduino to them to make them significantly more powerful.

In this first project, you will start with a commercially available robot without a lot of autonomous capability, and then, you'll add Arduino and a sonar sensor and expand the capability of the robot. The robot you'll start with is the Hexbug Spider, which is available at many toy stores and from most online retailers. For specifics, here's the website: www.hexbug.com/mechanical/spider/.

The following is an image of one such unit:

As this robot is very small, you're going to need a very small Arduino so that you don't load the system down too much. One possible choice is an extremely small implementation of Arduino, the TinyDuino. This is available at www.tiny-circuits.com. The following is an image of the TinyDuino processor board with a standard USB connector to give you some idea of the size:

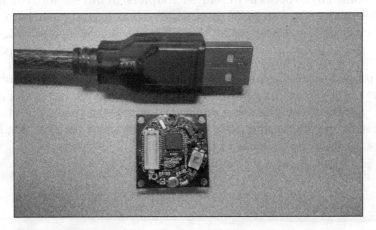

You'll need to order the USB programmer board as well so that you can program your TinyDuino. You'll also need some other additional pieces to complete this project. The Hexbug operates by controlling two motors. The first motor spins the top of the device, and when it stops, the spider will go in the new direction as defined by the new location. The other motor moves the spider forward and backward. Although the motors can go both directions, the motor that moves the top of the device goes a full 360 degrees, so you can drive both motors in the forward direction and your Hexbug can still go in any direction you'd like it to go. So, you can drive the Hexbug directly from Arduino (although if you'd like, you can add the motor driver board from TinyCircuits). You will need a proto board so that you can connect to the motors and access the sonar sensor. The TinyDuino provides one of these as well. You'll stack this on top of the TinyDuino and the USB interface board.

Perform the following steps to add Arduino to the Hexbug:

1. The first step is to open up the spider and disconnect the control board. Do this by first unscrewing the top plate in the same way you'd unscrew it to change the batteries on the spider. Then, take out the three screws that are part of the top plate and expose the insides of the robot. You'll find a small controller board with six connections. Two of these connections, the white and black wire combinations, go to the two motors that control the direction and the forward/backward motion of the spider. From the top plate comes a red and black wire that supplies the power. Cut these wires. This is what the bottom part of the robot should now look like:

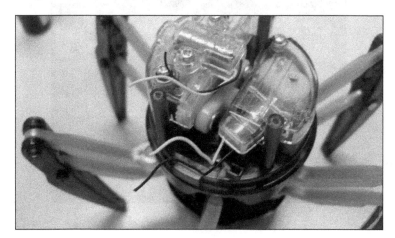

2. You'll want to add extension wires onto each of the six wires, so you can connect them to the TinyDuino that you'll mount on top of the robot. Once you have done this, route these wires out the hole to the left by removing the small controller board, and then reattach the top of the robot and the top plate.

3. You'll mount your TinyDuino and the associated shields on the top of the robot. You can do this by mounting the TinyDuino shields together using the TinyDuino mounting kit available at `tinycircuits.com`. However, you'll first want to solder some wires to the proto shield so that you can talk to the other sensors you'll want on the robot. For this project, you'll need to control two DC motors and the sonar sensor. The specifics for the sonar sensor were covered in *Chapter 8, Avoiding Obstacles Using Sensors*. Based on this information, you'll need access to pins 9 and 10 for the two motors and VCC, GND, and pins 12 and 11 for the sonar sensor.

4. You'll need to solder wires to the proto shield. The following is an image of the shield, which will give you an indication of where to add the wires:

5. When you have these wires attached to the proto board, you can connect all the TinyCircuits parts together. Now, you can start connecting the Hexbug to the TinyDuino. Let's start by controlling the two motors. You'll need to connect the rotating motor to pin 9 and GND and then connect the movement motor to pin 10 and GND on the proto board. You'll need to make several connections to the GND connection on the proto board, four to be exact, so you may want to make a four-to-one wire connector for this purpose. The following is an image of the board mounted and connected to the two motors:

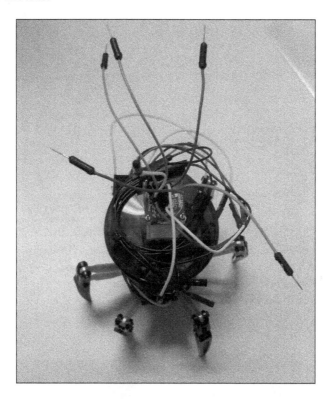

Now, let's try and see whether the spider's movement is again functional—this time, driven by the TinyDuino. To do this, you'll need to create just a bit of code:

```
int motor1 = 9;
int motor2 = 10;

void setup() {
  pinMode(motor1, OUTPUT);
  pinMode(motor2, OUTPUT);
}

void loop() {
  digitalWrite(motor1, HIGH);
  delay(500);
  digitalWrite(motor1, LOW);
  delay(1000);
  digitalWrite(motor2, HIGH);
  delay(500);
  digitalWrite(motor2, LOW);
}
```

When you upload the code, your robot should move forward slightly, then turn, move forward again, then turn, and so on. You can adjust the amount of movement and turn by changing the `delay (500);` statement in the code. Now, your robot can move around.

If you put a battery into the holder on the TinyDuino, your robot can even move when disconnected from the computer. I like to keep my USB connection board in this configuration; it makes it easier to hook up and modify the code.

Now, you can move around, but you'll certainly still bump into barriers. So, let's add the sonar sensor. To add the sensor, make the following connections:

Arduino pin	Sensor pin
5 V	VCC
GND	GND
12	Trig
11	Echo

You can mount your sonar sensor on the front of your Hexbug using velcro. The following is an image of the Hexbug with the sensor mounted:

Now, let's see whether the sensor is functional. Navigate to **Examples | NewPing | NewPingExample**. Select the **Serial Monitor** tab, and you should see the following screenshot:

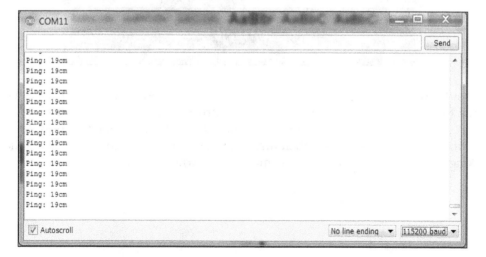

You can now sense barriers. It is straightforward to create a sketch that uses the motor control and sonar sensor. The following is a simple sketch that combines program statements for both, the DC motor control and sensor control:

```
hexspider | Arduino 1.0.5-r2

File Edit Sketch Tools Help

hexspider

#include <NewPing.h>

#define TRIGGER_PIN  12
#define ECHO_PIN     11
#define MAX_DISTANCE 200
int motor1 = 9;
int motor2 = 10;

NewPing sonar(TRIGGER_PIN, ECHO_PIN, MAX_DISTANCE);

void setup() {
  pinMode(motor1, OUTPUT);
  pinMode(motor2, OUTPUT);
  digitalWrite(motor1, HIGH);
  digitalWrite(motor2, LOW);
}

void loop() {
  int distance;
  delay(50);
  unsigned int uS = sonar.ping();
  distance = uS/ US_ROUNDTRIP_CM;
  if (distance > 0 && distance < 5)
    {
      digitalWrite(motor1, LOW);
      digitalWrite(motor2, HIGH);
      delay(1000);
      digitalWrite(motor2, LOW);
      digitalWrite(motor1, HIGH);
    }
  delay(1000);
}

Done Saving.
Binary sketch size: 1,948 bytes (of a 30,720 byte maximum)

26                        Arduino Pro or Pro Mini (3.3V, 8 MHz) w/ ATmega328 on COM11
```

The NewPing sonar(TRIGGER_PIN, ECHO_PIN, MAX_DISTANCE); statement sets up the sonar sensor so that it knows about the proper trigger and echo pins. In the setup() function, you are going to set the OUTPUT mode for the two pins that will control the DC motors and then turn one motor on (the motor that powers the walking) and the other motor off (the motor that turns the device).

The `loop()` function checks the sonar sensor using the `sonar.ping()` command. When the distance is greater than 0 and less than 5, you will turn the walking motor off, turn the turning motor on for one second, and then turn the turning motor off and turn the walking motor back on. When the spider encounters an object, the program should turn the walking motor off, turn the spider by about 90 degrees, and then turn the walking motor back on.

Now, upload your program. Your robot should now move forward, and when it senses a barrier, it stops and turns and then moves in the new direction. Your robot can move around and sense barriers! Implementing the intelligence to go between points A and B while avoiding barriers is an interesting and complex problem that you can now explore. There are algorithms that show how to program your robot to respond when it senses a barrier by moving efficiently around it. For more information on this, see `research.ncl.ac.uk/game/mastersdegree/gametechnologies/aipathfinding/AI%20Pathfinding%20Tutorial.pdf` and `biorob.epfl.ch/files/content/users/175246/files/Public/Pictures/ReportMaster.pdf`.

Now that you have learned how to build small robots, let's turn to an entirely different application for Arduino — fashion.

Wearable Arduino projects

In this section, you'll build projects that you'll wear as a part of your clothing or accessories. Hopefully, this will expand your concept of where you might be able to creatively use Arduino. Let's get started.

The project for this section is a wearable pin that will indicate your direction through a circular LED set. You could wear this type of device on an armband, like a watch, or pin it on your clothes, just to prove that you are not only technically savvy, but have a keen fashion sense. However, as we are talking about robots, you can actually add these wearables to your robot to give the outside world some indication of what the robot is thinking.

To start, you'll need an Arduino board built for fashion. For this project, you'll use the FLORA. This was introduced in *Chapter 1*, *Powering on Arduino*. It has a different form factor; it looks like the following image:

The Arduino FLORA unit is interesting for a couple of reasons. Its form factor is certainly one of them, but it is also designed to go into wearable applications and is even washable (but don't try it with the battery attached). In this particular application, you'll be using the FLORA with two of its accessories to build a device that can indicate direction. To do this, you'll need both a way of finding the direction as well as a way of indicating direction. To find direction, you'll add the FLORA Accelerometer/Compass module, the LSM303, available at www.adafruit.com. The following is an image of this device, with the FLORA on the right-hand side for size comparison:

This module was specifically designed to be used with the FLORA processor. For the indicator, you'll use the NeoPixel ring, which is also available at www.adafruit.com. This ring provides lighting in different colors. The following is an image of the ring, again with the FLORA on the right-hand side for size comparison:

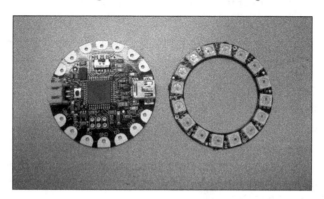

Perform the following steps to get the NeoPixel ring working with the FLORA:

1. First, make the following connections between the FLORA and the NeoPixel ring:

Flora pin	NeoPixel ring pin
VBATT	Power 5 V DC
GND	Power signal ground
D6	Data input

2. Now, you'll need to download, if you have not already done so, the Arduino IDE designed to work with the FLORA. You can download it from learn.adafruit.com/getting-started-with-flora/download-software.

3. After you have done this, you'll need to download the library from github.com/adafruit/Adafruit_NeoPixel.

4. Install this into the library directory of your Adafruit Arduino IDE.

5. Now, bring up a simple example program by navigating to **Examples | Adafruit_Neopixel | strandtest**.

Upload this program, and your NeoPixel ring should start displaying various colors. Now that the ring is working, let's add a digital compass to the project. Here are the steps:

1. You'll need to connect the digital compass to the FLORA. The following are the connections:

FLORA pin	LSM303
3.3 V	3 V
GND	Po
SDA	SDA
SCL	SCL

2. Now that you have made the connections, you'll need to download the library that supports the LSM303 device from `github.com/adafruit/Adafruit_LSM303DLHC`.

3. You'll also need to download and install Adafruit's sensor library from `github.com/adafruit/Adafruit_Sensor`.

4. When you have installed these, upload the digital compass example program by navigating to **Examples** | **Adafruit_LSM303DLHC** | **magsensor**. When you open the **Serial Monitor** tab, you should see the following screenshot:

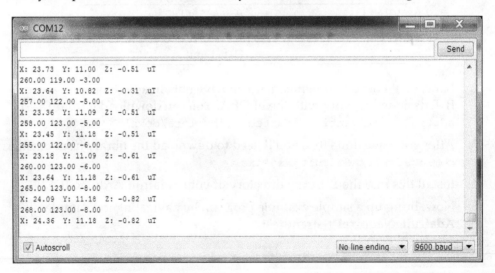

The device is reporting information on the direction. A more useful way to look at this data is provided by Adafruit at `learn.adafruit.com/lsm303-accelerometer-slash-compass-breakout/coding`. At the bottom of this page is a listing that will show the actual direction when the device is held flat. Unfortunately, you'll need to make just a couple of changes because of the updates to the drivers. The following is the new sketch:

Specifically, you'll need to change #include <Adafruit_LSM303.h> to #include <Adafruit_LSM303_U.h>. You'll also need to change Adafruit_LSM303_Mag mag = Adafruit_LSM303_Mag(12345); to Adafruit_LSM303_Mag_Unified mag = Adafruit_LSM303_Mag_Unified(12345);.

When you upload and run this program, and open the **Serial Monitor** tab, you should see the following screenshot:

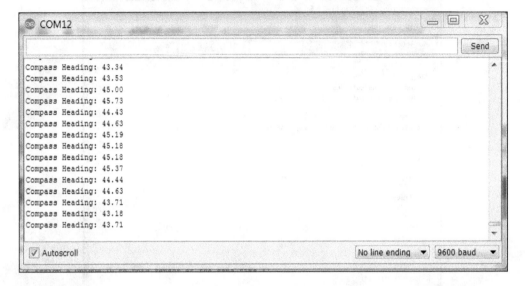

Now, you have access to Compass Heading. The final step is to merge the NeoPixel code with the Compass Heading code. The following is a simple example that changes color based on the direction:

```
Floracompass | Arduino 1.0.5
File Edit Sketch Tools Help

Floracompass §

#include <Wire.h>
#include <Adafruit_Sensor.h>
#include <Adafruit_LSM303_U.h>
#include <Adafruit_NeoPixel.h>
#define PIN 6
Adafruit_LSM303_Mag_Unified mag = Adafruit_LSM303_Mag_Unified(12345);
Adafruit_NeoPixel strip = Adafruit_NeoPixel(60, PIN, NEO_GRB + NEO_KHZ800);
void setup(void){
   Serial.begin(9600);
   Serial.println("Magnetometer Test"); Serial.println("");
   if(!mag.begin())
     Serial.println("Ooops, no LSM303 detected ... Check your wiring!");
   strip.begin();
   strip.show();
}
void loop(void){
   sensors_event_t event;
   mag.getEvent(&event);
   float Pi = 3.14159;
   float heading = (atan2(event.magnetic.y,event.magnetic.x) * 180) / Pi;
   if (heading < 0)  {
     heading = 360 + heading;
   }
   Serial.print("Compass Heading: ");
   Serial.println(heading);
   if (heading > 0 && heading < 90)
     colorWipe(strip.Color(255,0,0), 50);
   else if ( heading > 90 && heading < 180)
     colorWipe(strip.Color(0,255,0), 50);
   else if (heading > 180 && heading < 270)
     colorWipe(strip.Color(0,0,255), 50);
   else if ( heading > 270 && heading < 360)
     colorWipe(strip.Color(255,255,255), 50);
   delay(1000);
}
void colorWipe(uint32_t c, uint8_t wait) {
   for(uint16_t i=0; i<strip.numPixels(); i++) {
     strip.setPixelColor(i, c);
     strip.show();
     delay(wait);
   }
}

Done uploading.
Binary sketch size: 13,704 bytes (of a 28,672 byte maximum)

                                            Adafruit Flora on COM12
```

And there you have it! As you move your device around, you should see the color of the ring change. The only step left is to package the device. You can put the pieces together on a button or a write strap, or connect them directly to your robot, and your LED will give you an indication of the direction in which the robot is heading. You could easily change the sensor to one that measures temperature, distance, or light; the possibilities are almost endless.

Summary

That's it, but not really. There are so many more projects you can now tackle as you have the basic capability in hand. You learned how to build simple robots that can roam around on wheels and even walk on legs. You built robots that can sense barriers and communicate with the outside world wirelessly. You also built robots that can sail, swim underwater, and even fly. However, you've really only just begun. There is plenty of help out there as well and almost as many different forms of Arduino as there are projects. So, feel free to create.

Index

Thank you for buying
Arduino Robotic Projects

About Packt Publishing

Packt, pronounced 'packed', published its first book "*Mastering phpMyAdmin for Effective MySQL Management*" in April 2004 and subsequently continued to specialize in publishing highly focused books on specific technologies and solutions.

Our books and publications share the experiences of your fellow IT professionals in adapting and customizing today's systems, applications, and frameworks. Our solution based books give you the knowledge and power to customize the software and technologies you're using to get the job done. Packt books are more specific and less general than the IT books you have seen in the past. Our unique business model allows us to bring you more focused information, giving you more of what you need to know, and less of what you don't.

Packt is a modern, yet unique publishing company, which focuses on producing quality, cutting-edge books for communities of developers, administrators, and newbies alike. For more information, please visit our website: www.packtpub.com.

About Packt Open Source

In 2010, Packt launched two new brands, Packt Open Source and Packt Enterprise, in order to continue its focus on specialization. This book is part of the Packt Open Source brand, home to books published on software built around Open Source licenses, and offering information to anybody from advanced developers to budding web designers. The Open Source brand also runs Packt's Open Source Royalty Scheme, by which Packt gives a royalty to each Open Source project about whose software a book is sold.

Writing for Packt

We welcome all inquiries from people who are interested in authoring. Book proposals should be sent to author@packtpub.com. If your book idea is still at an early stage and you would like to discuss it first before writing a formal book proposal, contact us; one of our commissioning editors will get in touch with you.

We're not just looking for published authors; if you have strong technical skills but no writing experience, our experienced editors can help you develop a writing career, or simply get some additional reward for your expertise.

C Programming for Arduino

ISBN: 978-1-84951-758-4   Paperback: 512 pages

Learn how to program and use Arduino boards with a series of engaging examples, illustrating each core concept

1. Use Arduino boards in your own electronic hardware and software projects.

2. Sense the world by using several sensory components with your Arduino boards.

3. Create tangible and reactive interfaces with your computer.

4. Discover a world of creative wiring and coding fun!

Raspberry Pi Home Automation with Arduino

ISBN: 978-1-84969-586-2   Paperback: 176 pages

Automate your home with a set of exciting projects for the Raspberry Pi!

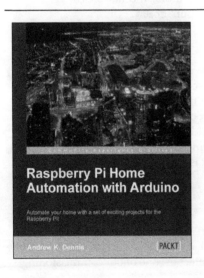

1. Learn how to dynamically adjust your living environment with detailed step-by-step examples.

2. Discover how you can utilize the combined power of the Raspberry Pi and Arduino for your own projects.

3. Revolutionize the way you interact with your home on a daily basis.

Please check **www.PacktPub.com** for information on our titles

Internet of Things with the Arduino Yún

ISBN: 978-1-78328-800-7 Paperback: 112 pages

Projects to help you build a world of smarter things

1. Learn how to interface various sensors and actuators to the Arduino Yún and send this data in the cloud.

2. Explore the possibilities offered by the Internet of Things by using the Arduino Yún to upload measurements to Google Docs, upload pictures to Dropbox, and send live video streams to YouTube.

BeagleBone Robotic Projects

ISBN: 978-1-78355-932-9 Paperback: 244 pages

Create complex and exciting robotic projects with the BeagleBone Black

1. Get to grips with robotic systems.

2. Communicate with your robot and teach it to detect and respond to its environment.

3. Develop walking, rolling, swimming, and flying robots.

Please check **www.PacktPub.com** for information on our titles